The Complete Book of

✤

WEDDING CRAFTS

First published in the United States of America by
Quarry Books, an imprint of
Rockport Publishers, Inc.
33 Commercial Street
Gloucester, Massachusetts 01930-5089
Telephone: (978) 282-9590
Fax: (978) 283-2742
www.rockpub.com

Library of Congress Cataloging-in-Publication data available

ISBN 1-59253-141-5

10 9 8 7 6 5 4 3 2 1

Production and Layout: Susan Raymond
Cover Images: Bobbie Bush Photography, Alan Penn Photography
Cover Design: Leigh Mantoni Stewart

Grateful acknowledgment is given to Bette Matthews for her work in *Wedding Invitations, Announcements, Place Cards, and More* (Rockport Publishers 2001) on pages 76–139; to April Paffrath and Laura McFadden for their work in *The Artful Bride* (Rockport Publishers 2003) on pages 6–29, 202–291, and 294–295, and for their work in *The Artful Bride: Wedding Invitations* (Quarry Books 2004) on pages 30–75 and 292–293; and to April Paffrath, Paula Grasdal, and Livia McRee for their work in *The Artful Bride: Wedding Favors and Decorations* (Quarry Books 2004) on pages 140–201 and 296–299.

Printed in China

The Complete Book of

✦

WEDDING CRAFTS

GLOUCESTER MASSACHUSETTS

QUARRY BOOKS

Contents

Introduction

A wedding is a romantic and special event for a couple. It is the culmination of a lot of planning—and a party you host for your family and friends. Creative and modern couples are often confronted with the option of warming over the traditional elements that find a home in everyone else's weddings. But we know you have your own sense of style. In everyday life, you expertly straddle social convention and your own personal flair. (For those who don't, there is Emily Post.) When it comes to weddings, however, women are confronted with demands from all sides, and a history that attempts to live up to Queen Victoria's legacy. (She started the white dress trend, after all.)

Clearly, not everyone gets married in Victoria and Albert style—or in Elvis' chapel of love. Most people fall somewhere in between. We've come up with ideas for the savvy middle group, with an occasional homage to either end of the spectrum. This book will provide ideas to help you create a wedding that has a real personality—your own.

photo by Bobbie Bush

A wedding has style only when it is infused with your ideas and humor. When you invite people to a wedding, you are throwing a great celebration for the people closest to you—the people who know you best. This is no time to cling to tired-out traditions or overdone details. Will the party be more fun if you add contrived elements to every aspect? Probably not—so leave the napkins alone.

The people you invite to your wedding know your sense of humor, your charm, and even your kooky taste in music. Don't be tempted to bury those qualities under layers of standard wedding elements. Create your own invitations, cards, favors, tiaras, and centerpieces. Consider how to adapt each item to your style and have a blast with it. Handmade wedding elements are fun to make, they give you greater control over the feel of your wedding, and they even provide you with some quality downtime during the preparation for the big day.

Correspondence

Correspondence is the first and last way you involve guests in your wedding. Your friends and family may not have even heard the marital buzz when invitations arrive in their mailboxes. And weeks later they are doubtless still talking about the amazing time they had celebrating when they receive a thank-you in the mail.

Invitations are the first clue guests have about what kind of a party you two are hosting. And, although strict adherents to etiquette bibles may shriek in horror, you can pick whatever you want to say and how to say it. Even Emily Post now agrees that an invitation does not have to be worded in the traditional manner. The year does not have to be spelled out and the "honour" of someone's presence can be requested in just about any way that reflects your personality. But, as an official invitation, it must include the crucial information: who, what, where, and when. Beyond that, the door is wide open to make the invitation memorable for more than fine engraving. Often the smallest weddings are announced with excited phone calls rather than a letterpress run of fifteen, so don't feel obligated to walk in other people's footsteps. In this chapter, we've included some examples that show how invitations can reflect different styles, using similar techniques. We also share some ways of packaging the invitation and essential information.

Thank-you notes are always in order. The fact that friends and family celebrated with you whole-heartedly is, in itself, a wonderful gift worthy of great thanks. That's not even to mention the assorted crystal, towels, paintings, vases, and toasters that may accompany your guests' earnest and personal well-wishes. Our thank-you ideas provide an elegant canvas for your note. As for writing the cards themselves, you and your sweetie should strive to stand out a little. It is very important to thank people for any gifts they have given you, but it is even more important to tell them what their presence meant to you. Go on, you can do it.

Mr. and Mrs. Howard Jones
request your presence
at the wedding of their daughter
Sarah Marie Jones
to
Michael J. McDonough
June 4, 2002
2 P.M.
Christ Church
40 Berwin Road
Newtowne, Pennsylvania
Reception to follow

The Right Buttons

INVITATION ENCLOSURE ENVELOPE

We can be pretty sure we're holding a wedding invitation in our hands when we open an envelope and find another tucked inside. Back in the days when footmen hand-delivered invitations of all sorts, the exterior envelope got messy from all the handling, while the interior enclosure stayed pristine. Now the mail carriers take care of the delivery, but the process is none the cleaner. An interior envelope remains the signal that we are opening something important. One way to make the enclosure envelope stand out and grab some attention is to make it feel and seal differently than other beautiful, traditional versions.

This two-toned vellum envelope looks elegant with its overlapping sheer colors and deckled edging. It is made whimsical and sweet by the button mechanism and the tiny photos of the two of you embedded in either button. To close the envelope, people tie the two of you together by winding a thread around the buttons. The sheer vellum invitation rests inside the flaps.

MATERIALS

8 1/2" × 11" (21.6 cm × 27.9 cm) sheets of pink and green vellum

4 3/4" × 6 1/2" (12.1 cm × 16.5 cm) pink vellum envelopes

8 1/2" × 11" (21.6 cm × 27.9 cm) sheets of white vellum for laser or inkjet printers

Personal computer

Photocopier or scanner and printer

Your favorite computer layout software

Pink embroidery thread

3/4" (1.9 cm)-wide shank buttons with a raised edge (that creates an inset for photos)

Deckled-edge decorative scissors

Bone folder

Craft knife

Scissors

Photos of you and your partner

Spray adhesive

Pencil

Template to match size of button inset

Pink sewing thread

Sewing needle

1. Fold the piece of 8 1/2" x 11" (21.6 cm x 27.9 cm) pink vellum in half, short sides together. Score the fold with a bone folder to make the edge crisp. Cut the long side down to 6" (15.2 cm) so that, folded, the paper measures 4 1/4" x 6" (10.8 cm x 15.2 cm).

2. Repeat the same process with the green vellum.

3. Lay folded pink vellum on work surface so that folded edge is on your right. Spray adhesive on the back of the pink vellum, the side that is touching the work surface. (Spray the adhesive in a separate, well-ventilated area. The glue will stick to everything on your work area otherwise.)

TIP *If you want to use 2-hole or 4-hole buttons instead of shank buttons, simply sew the buttons on first and then inset the photos.*

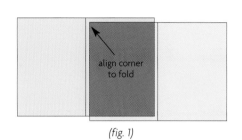

(fig. 1)

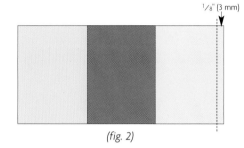

¹⁄₈" (3 mm)

(fig. 2)

4. Open up the green vellum sheet, like a book, and lay it flat. Adhere the sprayed side of the pink vellum to the green vellum this way: align the left edge of the sprayed panel with the fold line of the green vellum *(see fig. 1)*. The right edge of the green vellum should line up with the fold line of the pink vellum. Smooth out any bumps or bubbles with the bone folder.

5. Use a craft knife to cut another ¹⁄₈" (3 mm) from the free flap of the pink vellum *(see fig. 2)*.

6. Fold in the pink flap, then overlap with the free flap of the green. Score the folds with the bone folder to help the piece lay flat.

7. Open out the green vellum front cover flap. Measure and cut the green flap in half so it measures 2¹⁄₈" wide x 6" high (5.4 cm x 15.2 cm) as shown in *fig. 3*.

8. With a pencil, mark the center of the free edge of the green vellum *(see fig. 4)*. Make two other marks on the top and bottom of the flap, ¹⁄₂" (1.3 cm) in from folded edges.

9. Using a pencil and ruler, connect the top and bottom marks to the center mark, forming a pointed flap for the envelope.

10. With the decorative scissors, cut along pencil lines.

11. Reduce the photos to fit inside the buttons. You can do this at home with a scanner and printer, or you can take them to a copy center and have several made at once. Make sure you take a button with you to double-check the size. Do some experimenting at home with a plain piece of paper to make sure you get the correct size circles to nest into the buttons. Use a circle guide and a little trial-and-error. Ours worked well with a ⁵⁄₁₆" (8 mm) circle guide, but different buttons may vary.

12. Place a circle guide over the photos and draw a pencil line around the inside of the hole.

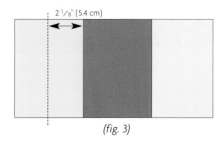
2 ¹/₈" (5.4 cm)

(fig. 3)

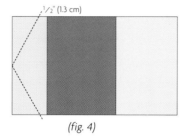
¹/₂" (1.3 cm)

(fig. 4)

13. Cut out photos with scissors and spray mount backs of photos. Inset photos into center of buttons.

14. Sew one button onto the green flap, about ¹/₂" (1.3 cm) in from point. Sew another button onto pink side, about ¹/₂" (1.3 cm) to the right of closed pointed flap.

15. Measure an 11" (27.9 cm) long strand of the pink embroidery thread and cut. Wrap around buttons.

TO MAKE THE INVITATION

1. Create a new document, 4¹/₈" x 6" (10.5 cm x 15.2 cm) in MS Word or your layout program.

2. Pick the font. We used Bernhard Tango 15 point.

3. Type your invitation and center the text.

4. Print invitation onto 8¹/₂" x 11" (21.6 cm x 27.9 cm) white vellum.

5. Cut out the invitation with craft knife and reopen button closure envelope. Place the invitation inside, close the envelope, and rewrap thread.

VARIATION *If you don't want to use photographs of yourselves in the button centers, try a monogrammed approach by using buttons with each of your initials on them.*

Say It with Flowers

PANSY ENVELOPE INVITATION

MATERIALS

8 ½" × 11"
(21.6 cm × 27.9 cm)
white vellum
for laser or
inkjet printers

Printer

Personal computer

Your favorite
computer layout
software

Pencil

Metal ruler

Drafting triangle

Craft knife

Hole punch

5 ¼" (13.3 cm)
square yellow
petal envelopes

Yellow and
white swirl paper

³/8" (1 cm)
light purple ribbon,
7" (17.8 cm)
per invitation

Scissors

Pansy stickers

Flowers deservedly have a prominent place in many weddings, because of their beauty and vitality. What better qualities to exalt on this occasion? This invitation is simple decorative paper packaged in a special envelope. The petal style of the envelope and the light yellow and purple colors of the materials make the entire invitation very springy. Seal it with a pansy sticker in the same color range.

1. With your favorite computer layout software, create your 4 ³/8" (11.1 cm) square invitation. Print onto 8 ½" x 11" (21.6 cm x 27.9 cm) vellum. Trim to size.

2. Measure and cut out a 5" (12.7 cm) square of the yellow and white swirl paper.

3. Place vellum on top of swirl paper and make two tick marks with your pencil, ½" (1.3 cm) from the top edge and 2 ¼" (5.7 cm) from both the left and right edges of the layered sheets.

4. Punch holes in marked areas. Tie the two sheets of paper together by knotting a 7" (17.8 cm) piece of light purple ribbon through the holes. Trim ends on a diagonal.

5. Place in petal envelope and seal envelope with a pansy sticker.

VARIATION *Place two faux wedding bands in the middle of the knot of purple ribbon, leaving enough space under the rings so the invitation wording is not covered up.*

PLEASE COME JOIN US
IN THE CELEBRATION OF
OUR WEDDING
KIM FURNALD
&
TIM GRAY
JUNE 8, 2003
1 P.M.
HILLISTON HISTORICAL SOCIETY
525 OLD CAMBRIDGE ROAD
HILLISTON, MA
RECEPTION TO FOLLOW

Time to RSVP

An invitation is a unique piece of mail. Layered materials give recipients plenty to experience. It lets them know that the occasion is special and attention-worthy. This invitation combines several decorative papers that open like a triptych to reveal a skeleton leaf and a sheer vellum invitation. The texture of the varied materials invokes the feeling you and your spouse-to-be are trying to create, whether it's sleek, folksy, ethereal, or something completely different. Spend some time perusing the paper choices until you find a combination that best represents your style.

1. With your favorite computer layout software, create your 3 ½" x 5 ¼" (8.9 cm x 13.3 cm) invitation. Print onto 8 ½" x 11" (21.6 cm x 27.9 cm) vellum. Trim to size.

2. Measure and cut out an 8 ½" wide x 6" (21.6 cm x 15.2 cm) piece of cream paper and decorative paper. Spray mount two sides together, decorative sides facing out.

3. Place cream side facing up. Measure and mark a vertical line with a pencil, 2 ¼" (5.7 cm) in on left and right sides of wide part of paper. Fold paper in on pencil lines with a bone folder. Erase pencil lines.

4. Open up cover and place vellum invitation inside, adhering it to the interior cream side of the cover with photo corners.

5. Place leaf over invitation and fold cover shut.

6. Cut a 25" (63.5 cm) length of ribbon and tie around outside with a bow.

TIP *When you select your paper, keep in mind the invitation size; a small pattern may have more impact than large, dynamic graphics.*

MATERIALS

8 ½" × 11"
(21.6 cm × 27.9 cm)
white vellum for
laser or inkjet printers

Printer

Personal computer

Your favorite computer
layout software

Pencil

Metal ruler

Drafting triangle

Craft knife

Bone folder

White eraser

4 ½" × 6 ¼"
(11.4 cm × 15.9 cm)
cream envelopes

Matching cream paper

Decorative paper

Tan skeleton leaves

Spray adhesive

Photo corners

1" (2.5 cm)
coordinating organdy
or organza ribbon

Eco-Invite

LEAF WINDOW INVITATION

MATERIALS

8 1/2" × 11"
(21.6 cm × 27.9 cm)
white vellum for
laser or inkjet printers

Printer

Personal computer

Your favorite computer
layout software

Pencil

Metal ruler

Drafting triangle

Craft knife

5 1/4" (13.3 cm)
square tan petal
envelopes

Green and tan
variegated
decorative paper

Green leaf
decorative paper

Small green
leaf skeletons

Spray adhesive

There are so many reasons to love this woodsy invitation. You don't have to be a hiker, an ecologist, or a weekend garden-partier, but you do have to like amazing forest tones and tree imagery. If you are getting married outdoors, this invitation is a natural (in so many ways).

If natural, recycled papers are important to you, you're in luck with this project. Some of the most popular natural options are the patterns and styles that best create this look.

1. With your favorite computer layout software, create your 10" wide x 5" high (25.4 cm x 12.7 cm) invitation. Design the text to fit on 5" x 5" (12.7 cm x 12.7 cm) area on the right side of the document. Print onto 8 1/2" x 11" (21.6 cm x 27.9 cm) vellum. Trim to size.

2. Measure and cut out a 10" x 5" (25.4 cm x 12.7 cm) piece of both the leaf paper and variegated paper. Spray mount two sides together, decorative sides facing out.

3. Place variegated side facing up. Measure and cut a 1 1/2" x 2" (3.8 cm x 5.1 cm) window, 1 3/4" (4.4 cm) from the right edge and 1 1/2" (3.8 cm) from the top edge of the paper.

4. Flip the paper over so the leafy side is facing up. Spray the leafy side of paper with spray adhesive. Adhere vellum invitation to leafy side of paper. Make sure the invitation words are to the right of the window and do not overlap the opening. Fold invitation in half so it measures 5" (12.7 cm) square.

5. Close the invitation. Spray the back of the skeleton leaf with adhesive and place in center of window.

VARIATION *You don't have to use two different decorative papers. You can skip the inside paper, if you like the look of the "wrong" side of the main paper. The process will be simpler, but the look may not be as finished as with two designs.*

We're getting hitched!
Our joy will be more complete
if you celebrate with us.
Nimali Jacobson
&
Hermes Fernands
Saturday, October 6, 2003
4 p.m.
St. Thomas Church
New York, New York

Material World

The vibrant color and lush silver on this invitation recall a history of marking celebrations with decadent materials and intricate handiwork. Fabrics add dynamic colors and patterns, as well as a textural layer, to your invitation. The project is simple, but the combination of textures makes it feel intricate.

1. With your favorite computer layout software, create your 3 ½" x 5 ½" (8.9 cm x 14 cm) invitation. Print onto 8 ½" x 11" (21.6 cm x 27.9 cm) vellum. Trim to size.

2. Measure and cut out a 4" x 6" (10.2 cm x 15.2 cm) piece of corrugated paper. Center vellum on top of corrugated paper and place a tick mark with your pencil ¾" (1.9 cm) from top and 2" (5.1 cm) from the left (this should be dead center, left to right). Make a hole through the two layers with a hole punch.

3. Drop your eyelet grommet through the hole so decorative side of grommet faces front of the invitation. Place invitation layers face down and place eyelet setting tool through back of hole. Hit punch with a hammer so edges of eyelet flange outward. Once edges have flanged, hit back of eyelet again until edges flatten.

4. To make cover: Measure and cut out a 10" wide x 6" (25.4 cm x 15.2 cm) piece of material gift wrap. Lay flat horizontally, wrong side up. Measure in 3" (7.6 cm) from the sides on both sides and draw a pencil line to mark. Fold inward on pencil line and score edges with a bone folder.

5. On the left flap, place a tick mark with your pencil ¼" (6.4 mm) in from flap edge and 3" (7.6 cm) from the top. Make a hole with a hole punch.

6. Place the grommet through the hole, decorative side out. Finish grommet as in step three.

7. Place finished invitation inside material sleeve and tie with a tassel. The tassel will not fit through the eyelet hole so follow this procedure: Push a small loop of tassel cord through the back of the eyelet, and out through the front of the cover flap. Make a loop in other tie end and tie the two loops in a bow.

VARIATION *This format can be used for more than invitations. Try a fabric treatment for a reception dinner menu or a program of events. Guests unwrap the tassel tie to see what is written inside.*

MATERIALS

**8 ½" × 11"
(21.6 cm × 27.9 cm)
white vellum for
laser or inkjet printers**

Printer

Personal computer

**Your favorite computer
layout software**

**Wavy, silver
corrugated paper**

Pencil

Metal ruler

Drafting triangle

Craft knife

**3 mm eyelet
grommets**

Hole punch

Eyelet setting tool

Hammer

**Stiff Indian
material gift wrap
(decorative paper
can be substituted)**

Bone folder

Tassels with strings

Flocking Together

ORIGAMI ANNOUNCEMENT

MATERIALS

**Origami
paper squares**

**¹/₄" (6.4 mm)
wide satin ribbon**

**Thread that
matches the
ribbon color**

Sewing needle

**Personal
computer**

Printer

**Your favorite
computer
layout software**

Scissors

Envelope

**Decorative
straw**

You want a tradional announcement? You know where Crane's is located, friends. There's nothing wrong with that at all—it's one of our favorite stationers. But what about creative and amusing, or even a little out of the ordinary? That you're going to have to do yourself, with no help from the kings of kid-finish paper.

Finding a new type of announcement can be a little daunting. We relied on a history of amazing, but easy, origami to create a mailable vignette to herald the news. Three-dimensional items can be tricky to send through the postal service, so it helps to keep things small and basic. We thought a bird of a simple feather would travel well.

1. With your favorite computer layout software, create a box 2 ⅛" wide x 2 ¼" high (5.4 cm x 5.7 cm). Type your announcement text in the box, using your favorite typeface.

2. Print out as many copies as announcements to send. Cut out each printout.

3. Roll each piece of paper and tie with a 3" (7.6 cm) piece of ribbon.

4. Lay the square of origami paper, decorative side up. Fold the paper in half once, point to point. Unfold, leaving a crease down the middle (see fig. 1).

5. Flip the paper over. Fold the left and right corners to the middle crease, aligning the paper edges along the crease (see fig. 2).

6. Fold the entire figure in half along the original crease. Fold the tip of the paper to the front, then to the back. Then unfold leaving a crease (see fig. 3).

VARIATION *Use two pieces of origami paper for a unique contrast. Place wrong sides together, use spray mount to hold them together if needed. The contrasting pattern will show on the bird's tail.*

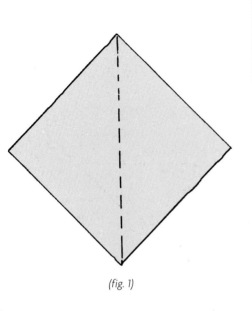

(fig. 1)

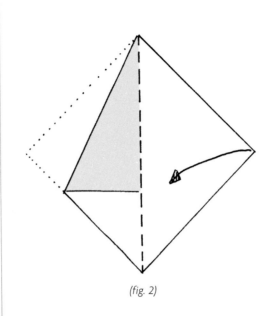

(fig. 2)

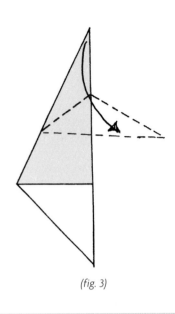

(fig. 3)

7. Invert the fold along the point, using the creases from step six. The result should look a little like a rabbit ear *(see fig. 4)*.

8. Follow the same strategy further up the point. Fold to the front, then fold to the back, then unfold, leaving a crease *(see fig. 5)*.

9. Repeat the same inversion further up the point to form the head of the bird *(see fig. 6)*.

10. Lay the bird flat and fold up the top layer of the body to meet with the "back." Flip over and repeat on the other side *(see fig. 7)*.

11. With the needle and thread, attach the ribbon-tied scroll to the beak of the bird. Double the thread so it will not break in transit.

12. Fold the bird flat, and package in an envelope with some decorative straw.

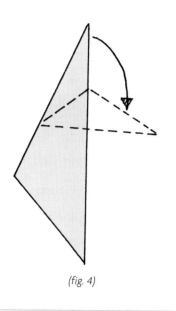

(fig. 4)

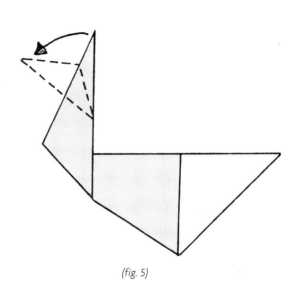

(fig. 5)

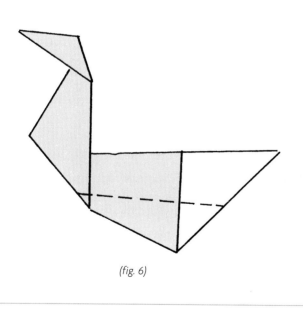

(fig. 6)

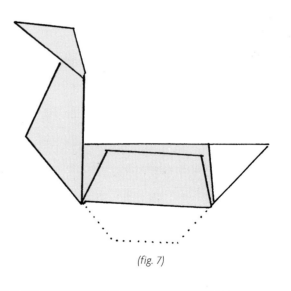

(fig. 7)

Blossoming Thanks

3D NOTE CARDS

MATERIALS

Small photo pebbles

Personal computer
and color printer
or photocopier

Plain white paper

Adhesive paper
flowers and stems

Plain 5 5/16" × 3 13/16"
(13.5 cm × 9.7 cm)
note cards

8 1/2" × 11"
(21.6 cm × 27.9 cm)
vellum paper

Craft knife

Decorative-edge
scissors

4" × 5"
(10.2 cm × 12.7 cm)
envelopes

PVA glue

Spray mount
adhesive

Inexpensive
paintbrush

Bone folder

Template from
page 294

Elaborate-looking thank-you notes don't necessarily take forever to make. Nor do you have to buy them in packs of ten. These flower cards are a matter of simple assembly-line construction—but their effect is anything but plain. Using photo pebbles, your thanks are magnified and stand out from the usual notes available.

When your hand is cramping after writing what feels like the five thousandth card, prevent your tuckered hand from giving the wrong impression. The liquid ink used in roller ball and fountain pens will make your handwriting appear smoother than a ballpoint pen, which shows every shake. If you're unfamiliar with fountain pens, practice writing your to-do lists with them. Think smooth.

1. Color copy the template from page 294 or print "thanks" logos onto plain white paper. You can also create your own design using your favorite computer layout software or handwrite them with permanent ink.

2. With a paintbrush, spread a thin layer of PVA on the flat surface of the photo pebble and center over the "thanks" image. To ensure the image doesn't run, do not move the photo pebble once you've put it in place. Wait for the glue to set (about 10 minutes).

3. Cut out the paper around the pebble with a craft knife, removing extraneous paper.

4. Spray mount colored vellum onto the note card and smooth out any bubbles with the bone folder. Fold paper in half along the natural fold of the note card. Score the fold with the bone folder.

5. Trim note card and paper with the decorative-edged scissors.

6. Adhere paper flower and stem to the center of the card.

7. Glue the pebble to the center of the flower.

TIP *If you are creating your own "thanks" images, experiment with the photo pebble to make sure the finished product is legible—the photo pebble magnifies the word and can cut off the image edges if the letters are too large.*

Budgeting Time

Photographer/Artist: Monica Lau, Getty Images

We cannot say this enough: Start early. More importantly: Finish early. Plenty of things can be frustrating when planning a wedding, but very little has to be. Do everything you can to eliminate the difficulties that come with running out of time. That frustration is the main reason many people hire consultants to do everything for them, figuring that it's better to lose money than to lose your cool. But, you may not need to decide between the two, if you keep time in mind. Granted, no amount of help we or anyone else offer can eliminate chilly feet or a lifetime of communication difficulties with your mother. If these are problems you've got, find a consultant and a stack of post-its and mark your favorite pages of this book for him or her so you can focus on other things.

SET YOUR OWN EXPECTATIONS

If you expect everything to run smoothly and turn out perfectly, chances are you won't believe anyone who warns you about being disappointed. If you set unrealistic expectations for yourself, you will be agitated in trying to achieve them, and your chances of having fun diminish greatly. Who wants that? On the other hand, don't believe anyone who says you must get stressed out and reach a breaking point—that's absolute baloney! If you feel unstressed, look at it as a blessing and enjoy the time. It's good to feel satisfied with the plans you've made and the work you've done. Forcing yourself to stress about it will not make your wedding more charming, but it will have an adverse effect on you. It's better to have great memories of your wedding *and* the time leading up to it.

The first step to getting things done on time and done well is to acknowledge that there are intermediate points between perfection and failure. A project that looks beautiful but isn't devoid of flaws is not a failure, it's handmade. Allow yourself to capture the spirit of your relationship, without getting bogged down by perfection anxiety.

TRY PROJECTS OUT

You'll have a greater success with projects if you try them out well in advance. Try out all the projects you are contemplating. Use the ones that turn out best and leave the less-than-gorgeous ones behind. You're committing to a person, not a style of photo frame.

KNOW WHEN TO LET THINGS GO

Most people hire help of some sort for their wedding. Whether it's a florist, a caterer, a restaurant, or judge, choose the people or organizations carefully so you can feel confident about their abilities. The more at ease you are with those providing a service, the more removed you can be from the minutiae. You and your fiancé should convey to everyone involved your desires for each element of the day. Then decide what amount of deviation from your ideal you are willing to accept. Elements you don't want to change will require closer managing. Likewise, if you are unsure about anyone's abilities, you will have to spend more time and energy supervising. If you can handle giving talented people some freedom, it is the best situation to hire people who do a fantastic job and to give them the space to do it.

Sometimes quality relates to budget—but not always. You will have to find the right balance for you. If you are short on time, it can be much better to spend a little more for a super florist than to waste valuable hours going over a plan time and again—or worse, dealing with a floral "catastrophe" on your wedding day.

Letting capable people fully control their roles allows you time to devote as you choose. Perhaps that allows you to arrive at your wedding unfrazzled. Or maybe it frees up enough time for you to leisurely make place cards (see pages 272, 288, 290), mini photo albums (see page 208), and decorative photo frames (see pages 204, 220, 290) for all your guests. ✳

Please join us in the
celebration of our love

Carlos Santiago
&
Birthe Cruetz

Saturday May 29, 2004

4 o'clock p.m.

Church of the Transfiguration

West Collingswood, New Jersey

Reception to follow

Arts and Crafts Style

VERTICAL ARTISAN INVITATION

William Morris was headed for a life in the church before turning to art and becoming one of the one of the earliest movers and shakers in the Arts and Crafts movement. Elevating craftsmanship to a fine art, Morris worked with a band of talented people, such as Burne-Jones and Rossetti, creating works of all kinds, from furniture to windows to tiles. Morris's most well-known type of creation influenced this design—his intricate and complex wallpapers. A simple invitation on plain paper is wrapped in a swath of detailed floral paper and tied with a coordinating ribbon. This invitation is nested inside an end-opening envelope that makes the most of the vertical orientation—and makes it feel like anything but business.

DIRECTIONS

1. Using your favorite page layout program, create a new document 8 ½" × 11" (22 cm × 28 cm).

2. Draw a box 3 ¾" wide × 9" deep (9.5 cm × 23 cm). Set the type for your invitation in the box, leaving a 1 ¾" (4.5 cm) margin at the top and bottom. (We used 14 point Amphora on leading of 23 points. Color the text dark green.)

3. Once you've perfected the first invitation, copy and paste an additional one right next to the original. This way you'll be able to run two up, side by side on the 8 ½" × 11" (22 cm × 28 cm) sheet.

4. Print the invitations out on the 8 ½" × 11" (22 cm × 28 cm) cream-colored card stock (you may first want to test this out on white printer paper to make sure you like the way it looks).

VARIATION *For a more vibrant look, this can also be made with salmon-colored stock to match the salmon-colored envelopes.*

MATERIALS

4 ⅛" × 9 ⅛" (10.3 cm × 23.3 cm) salmon-colored envelope with flap on long end

8 ½" × 11" (22 cm × 28 cm) coordinating cream-colored cover stock

8 ½" × 11" (22 cm × 28 cm) or larger sheet of decorative paper

deckled edged scissors or rotary paper trimmer with deckled-edge attachment

¼" wide × 15" long (0.5 cm × 38 cm) of coordinating ribbon

personal computer

page layout program (such as Quark or PageMaker)

color printer

triangle

pencil

metal ruler

craft knife

bone folder

scissors

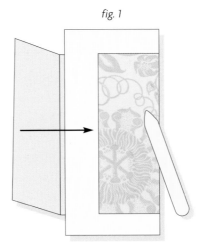

fig. 1

5. Trim the invitation with your rotary cutter or utility knife and ruler.

6. Place a sheet of the decorative paper, face down, on your cutting surface. Draw a rectangle 11" wide × 6" deep (28 cm × 15 cm). Trim paper to size with craft knife.

7. Deckle the edges of the wide side of the paper with rotary trimmer or deckled-edged scissors.

8. Assemble the invitation. Place paper on work surface decorative side down *(see fig. 1)*. Place cream-colored invite face up in center of the wide side of the decorative paper. Fold left over right sides of decorative paper into the center of the invitation and score each side with bone folder.

9. Tie ribbon in a knot and trim excess with scissors.

10. Insert in salmon-colored envelope.

TIP *When using a complex paper pattern, choose your ribbon carefully. You want colors to mesh, but too much detail in the ribbon, like a pattern of its own, steals the oomph of the gorgeous paper you've picked. Save the elaborate ties for use with simple papers.*

Curvy Embrace

INTERLOCKING ENCLOSURE

The inspiration for this invitation comes from a hefty, lovely purchase on Madison Avenue (of course). Actually, the purchase itself was weighty crystal, but the real spark of this idea came from the receipt. That's right. Sometimes, swanky *objets* at high-end boutiques result in elaborate proofs of purchase (who wants to look at paper from a register when there are goodies in the bag, for heaven's sake?). Their lovely receipt enclosure was quite different from this invitation, but the idea is the same: curvy forms of paper that interlock to cradle the enclosed paper. We used chocolate brown and violet to mimic the lovely window display in a pâtisserie.

DIRECTIONS

1. Cut two 5" × 11" (13 cm × 28 cm) pieces of cover-weight paper.

2. Cover 5" (13 cm) of one end of each piece of paper with spray adhesive. Align the sprayed sections of the papers and firmly press together so that the pieces overlap exactly 5" (13 cm), making a long, thin strip.

3. Using the bone folder, score the paper at each edge of the 5" (13 cm) overlap. Enlarge the template from page 293 to 200 percent. Align the template with the scored edges. Cut along the template guide, making sure to cut in far enough where the circles meet (the cut should extend just past a point 2 ½" (6 cm) from the scored line).

4. Fold the flaps inward on the score line, using a bone folder to make the folded edges crisp.

5. Using your computer, create a 4 ⅞" (12 cm) document and set your invitation wording. We used 10 point Colonna MT text on leading of 22 points. Coordinate your font color with enclosure colors. Print document onto blue card-weight paper. Trim the invitation document using scalloped edge of rotary trimmer or scalloped paper edger scissors.

6. Use a small amount of glue at the top of enclosure and adhere the invitation paper. Interlock the circles to close the invitation.

7. Tie a coordinating ribbon around the finished invitation enclosure.

VARIATION *For more contrast between the interlocking panels, use two colors for the enclosure instead of one.*

MATERIALS

8 ½" × 11"
(22 cm × 28 cm)
brown stardream
cover weight paper

8 ½" × 11"
(22 cm × 28 cm)
blue card stock

scissors

paper cutter

rotary trimmer with scalloped-edge blade or paper edger scissors

bone folder

spray adhesive

glue stick

personal computer

page layout software (such as Quark or PageMaker)

color printer

template from page 293

12" (30 cm) length of blue silk ribbon

What the Buzz Is About

DRAGONFLY POP-UP INVITATION

MATERIALS

2 sheets 8 ½" × 11"
(22 cm × 28 cm)
lavender card stock

36" (91 cm) -long pieces
of organdy ribbon
in lavender,
pale green, and gold

1 piece 8 ½" × 11"
(22 cm × 28 cm) pale
green vellum

1 piece 8 ½" × 11"
(22 cm × 28 cm)
gold vellum

dragonfly stamp

stamping inks in
green and gold

gold marker

2 head pins

2 tiny blue beads

2 tiny
turquoise beads

wire cutters

craft knife

6" × 8 ¾"
(15 cm × 22.5 cm)
envelope

¹/₈"-wide (.3 cm)
double-sided tape

PVA glue

The dragonfly, with its opalescent colors and diaphanous wings, has long been a staple of art and folklore. Throughout the world, the dragonfly represents a plethora of characteristics, from mischief-maker to symbol of happiness and strength. For this particular purpose, we're partial to the Native American Zuni tale of the helpful dragonfly who became an important messenger. In this invitation he is a messenger of great news. Whatever the symbology, the long lines of the dragonfly recall the easy days at the height of summer. The purple and green tones echo an earthy, natural attitude and simplicity.

DIRECTIONS FOR INVITATION

1. Fold an 11"-wide × 8 ½"-high (28 cm × 22 cm) lavender card stock in half vertically, using a bone folder to make a neat fold.

2. From another piece of lavender card stock, cut a rectangle 4" wide × 1 ½" high (11 cm × 4 cm). Fold in half vertically away from you to make a "mountain" crease, unfold, then measure ½" (1 cm) from each end and fold under (you should have a ½" by 1 ½" (1 cm × 4 cm) piece folded under).

3. Inside the 11" × 8 ½" (28 cm × 22 cm) card, mark a spot 4" (10 cm) from the left and right sides of the card and using double-sided tape, attach the two folded-under edges to the card, with crease centered, and centered from top to bottom. Crease should form a "mountain" to the "valley" formed by the card itself when the invitation is closed a little bit *(see fig. 1 on page 38)*.

VARIATION *The dragonfly was once the symbol of Japan, "the dragonfly island." Evoke that symbolism by shifting your color scheme slightly to white, black, and crimson.*

Katherine Winters

and

Gregory Gibeault

would be delighted

to have you share

in the joy of their marriage

Saturday, the fifth of July

at half after four o'clock

and afterward for dinner

and dancing under the stars

Oakleaf Arboretum

French Creek, Pennsylvania

Kindly reply by the fifth of June

M

will _____ attend the wedding

PROJECT DESIGN: ANDREA RENZI MCFADDEN

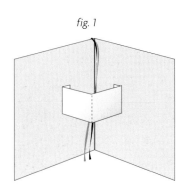

fig. 1

4. On scraps of lavender card stock, lightly tap or drag your stamp pad to add a green ink glaze. Let dry, then stamp two dragonflies with gold ink. Let dry and then use craft knife to cut out.

5. Put a dab of glue on each bead, and thread one bead onto each head pin. Trim pins with wire cutters so they are only ½" (1 cm) long. Use glue to attach pins to back of each dragonfly, so that only "eyes" show from the front. When glue is dry, crease dragonfly wings slightly to imitate real wings. Use double-sided tape to attach one to each side of the creased pop-up. Place them so they look as though they are about to kiss!

6. On an 11" wide × 8 ½" high (28 cm × 22 cm) piece of paper, print your invitation so that it appears on the left 5 ½" × 8 ½" (14 cm × 22 cm) panel in landscape view. Crease in half vertically. Using a pencil, draw a light line ¼" (.5 cm) from right side, and using the line as a guide, trim the right edge of the paper with scalloped craft scissors. Line the trimmed edge with the gold marker.

7. Crease a piece of pale green 11" wide × 8 ½" high (28 cm × 22 cm) vellum in half vertically. Using a pencil, draw a light line ½" (1 cm) from right side, and using the line as a guide, trim the right edge of the paper with scalloped craft scissors.

8. Line up three pieces of ribbon. Pull all three through the "tunnel" formed by the pop-up in the card and then lay the card pop-up down on the table. Put the invitation on, then layer the vellum. Bring ribbons together and tie in a bow to hold layers together. Stamp a few gold dragonflies on vellum around the invitation. Let dry. On inside of card, stamp more dragonflies in gold and green flying around the page. You can also make some look like they are flying off the edge.

9. Line the envelope with a piece of gold vellum trimmed to fit. Stamp dragonflies randomly on return envelope, avoiding areas for addressing.

DIRECTIONS FOR RSVP CARD

1. Print "RSVP" on 5 ½" wide × 4" high (14 cm × 10 cm) lavender paper. Using a pencil, draw a light line ¼" (0.5 cm) from bottom edge, and using the line as a guide, trim the right edge of the paper with scalloped craft scissors.

2. Stamp two dragonflies. Line the trimmed edge with the gold marker. Attach with double-edged tape to card stock. Stamp dragonflies randomly on return envelope, avoiding the address area.

RSVP MATERIALS

5 1/2" wide × 4" high (14 cm × 10 cm) lavender card stock

envelope

dragonfly stamp

stamping inks in green and gold

gold marker

4 1/4" × 5" (10.5 cm × 13 cm) envelope

It's Not Your Whole Life

KEEPING THINGS IN PERSPECTIVE

Obviously, we think that the world of invitations holds great promise—after all, we've compiled a book all about those nuptial missives. Because we are thrilled by the potential creativity invitations offer, we are well aware of how consuming they can be. Add to that the cultural tendency to dive head-first into wedding planning without checking the water depth and you have the makings of energy deflation, frustration, and inundation. Not good. You deserve much better (and so does everyone around you).

Take it all in perspective. A wedding is a fabulous thing—and we do mean fabulous—but a life is even better. A wedding is a prelude to a marriage, after all, and the second part is more important. Don't get caught up in ceremonial details and forsake all that has made you stylish, savvy, and inimitable all along.

Throwing a gigantic party can be intimidating, and it's somewhat normal to obsess about the direction of the event and the details that make it stand out. Most engagements last from six months to one year. When is the last time you spent ten months planning a party? True, you probably want it to be quite a bit more special than your Friday evening progressive cocktail parties, but that does not mean that every moment of the many months until the happy event needs to be filled with plans, ideas, and conversations about it. You should be able to fall asleep at night thinking about something besides "the big day." It may take a little bit of work, but teach yourself how to incorporate the planning into your normal life. Wedding planning is not a hobby, and it would be a shame to replace your usual activities, nights out, parties, and yoga classes completely with a world of typefaces, color schemes, and guest lists.

It may be difficult when your loved ones want to hear the latest incarnation of your plans. But it is essential to keep your wits and wittiness about you. Keep in mind that your wedding takes up a single day in your life—or an entire weekend at the most. After it is over, you have the rest of your life ahead. Can you bear to have spent every conversation and waking moment thinking about this one day, with no thought to the weeks and months after? We didn't think so. And it's not your fault if you slide in that direction. We live in a culture where the planning of a wedding gets inflated monumentally, and that's a lot of pressure for one single day to handle. Have fun with the planning and the conversations, but mix it into your regular existence and your usual personality. Share your excitement with people, but remember to leave yourself room to get excited about other things as well.

If you get stuck in a wedding whirlpool, try the following:

- Have a discussion about the state of politics in some town, state, or country (as you once did before you started planning).
- Go shopping for shoes and makeup that you won't be wearing on your wedding day.
- Plan a non-honeymoon vacation with your soon-to-be-spouse that will take place three months after you get married.
- Institute a "wedding talk" jar. When you need a break from the pressures and constancy of planning, put a quarter in the jar for each time you infringe on your own limits.
- Tell friends who won't let the subject drop that you love that they are excited, but you need to talk about regular stuff for a bit.

Invitations are one of the first items to be tackled when planning a wedding. Because they set the tone for the event to come and give guests a first glimpse of what lies ahead, they can be a major drain on the amount of energy you've allotted to wedding planning. That's why we've tried to come up with many ideas to spur your own creativity and help you maximize your time and efforts. Invitation planning and production can be enjoyable, relaxing, rewarding, and even a little meditative. However, it can just as easily turn into an indecision fest where papers, fonts, and colors confuse you. Take it easy. Make a simple plan, and have fun with your creation. Learn when to let something go. Making an invitation design overly complex will result in an unfocused piece that has no style or impact. Go for a reflection of your own personalities and let it stop there. And in the end, as important as an invitation's role is in the whole process, it isn't the most important thing. What you two feel like after the wedding weighs a lot more heavily on that scale.

Bride in a Can

SPRINGY BRIDAL SURPRISE

Sometimes, a wedding invitation is a surprise. This one *really* is. Remember the joke can of salted nuts that really held coiled spring snakes to shock unsuspecting friends? This invitation works on the same idea. The reference to the old joke as well as the quirky humor makes this invitation a gem.

DIRECTIONS FOR BRIDE

1. Place the 3" (8 cm) piece of cardboard under the bottom of the spring and trace around the shape to form a circle.

2. Cut out the cardboard circle.

3. Cut a 4" (10 cm) square of tulle.

4. Fold the tulle in half. Then place the cardboard into the center of the tulle as shown (*see fig. 1 on page 44*).

5. Place tulle and cardboard composite into the second coil of the spring (*see fig. 2*) and sew to spring parameter.

6. Cut a rectangle of cotton fabric measuring 20" long × 2 ½" wide (51 cm × 6 cm).

7. Fold fabric in half vertically.

8. Iron fabric and pin sides as shown (*see fig. 3*).

9. Create a sheath by sewing seams ¼" (0.5 cm) in on pinned sides and turn right-side out, keeping sewn seams inside. One end should be left completely open.

10. Iron flat.

VARIATION *You could also use this for a bridal shower invitation or a card to give to a bride and groom.*

MATERIALS

3" (8 cm) square piece of cardboard

pencil

scissors

cupcake topper bride

6" long × 2 ¼" wide (15 cm × 5.5 cm) aluminum bottle

dismantled "snake in a can" spring

5" wide (13 cm) tulle ribbon

sewing needle

white sewing thread

small silk flower

¼" (0.5 cm) pink rhinestone (optional)

¼ yard (0.23 m) lightweight white cotton fabric

sewing machine

iron

personal computer

page layout software (such as Quark or PageMaker)

pearlescent printer paper

printer

decorative paper

craft knife

metal ruler

craft glue

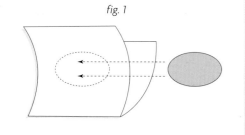

fig. 1

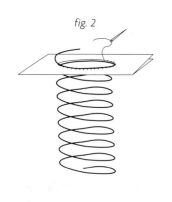

fig. 2

11. Place spring inside sheath, leaving sewn cardboard and tulle composite closest to open end of sheath *(see fig. 4)*.

12. Place cupcake bride into the center of the coil, so she stands on tulle and cardboard composite. Make sure seam of sheath is lined up with her back.

13. Tuck in frayed edges of fabric around top.

14. Double thread needle with about a 12-inch (30 cm) length of white thread and tie a knot at the end. Starting at seam of sheath, baste around the top of the sheath going in and out through tucked-over edge and exterior edge and pull tight to form a gather around bride's waist *(see fig. 5)*.

15. Secure skirt onto bride by sewing around holes in her arms.

16. Tie a knot at back of sheath, which is now her skirt.

17. Cut out a 5" × 8" (13 cm × 20 cm) rectangle of tulle and repeat steps 13 and 14 to form second layer of dress.

18. Tie a silk flower around her waist and secure wire around flower.

fig. 3

fig. 4

fig. 5

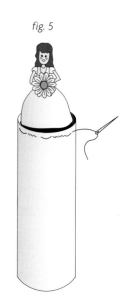

DIRECTIONS FOR RSVP

1. Using your favorite page layout program, create a document 10" wide × 4" deep (25 cm × 10 cm). Create a light pink box with a $\frac{1}{4}$" (0.5 cm) border of white all around.

2. Draw a dotted vertical line 5" (13 cm) from left edge. Insert the scissors character from the Zapf Dingbat font along the dotted line and set the text "cut along fold line and mail back postcard" going up the side of the line.

3. Scan template for corners (shown right) as a .tiff at 100 percent and paste them into your document at corners of pink box as accents.

4. Create a 65 percent black block 2 $\frac{1}{4}$" × 4" (5.5 cm × 10 cm) and set wedding invitation in center in white type (we used 7 point Eurostile on leading of 22 points). Center it in the 5-inch wide (13 cm) space.

5. Set "RSVP" on the right side of the card as shown in photo (ours is 6 point Eurostile on leading of 22 points).

6. Print and trim invite.

7. Cut out a 10" × 4" (25 cm × 10 cm) piece of decorative paper.

8. Spray adhere back of 10" × 4" (25 cm × 10 cm) printed invite to wrong side of 10" × 4" (25 cm × 10 cm) decorative paper.

9. Fold in half.

10. For RSVP, create a label to write the address on the decorative side. Either handwrite name or use Avery label system.

*template for
decorative corners*

VARIATION *The aluminum cans may get expensive. A cheaper alternative is a cardboard mailing tube.*

Bottle of Bliss
INVITATION DESERT-ISLE STYLE

MATERIALS

½ tablespoon sand

flexible bead needle

24" (61 cm) turquoise
embroidery floss

scissors

one ¼" (2 cm)
seashell

several tiny seashells,
beach glass, and
small crystal beads

bottle
7" × 1⅛" × 1⅛"
(18 cm × 4 cm × 4 cm)

one cork

craft glue

4 small
pearl beads

4 seashells with
holes drilled

4 medium
fish beads

6 small
crystal beads

6 tiny
blue beads

8 tiny
turquoise beads

4 medium
blue beads

2 medium
turquoise beads

No, you're not stranded anywhere. Far from it. This beaded bottle stuffed with a coiled invitation evokes the feeling of a tropical paradise. It works perfectly with a beach wedding . . . think casual linens for the entire wedding party, bare feet or sandals you kick off at the kiss. Let people know what kind of festivity they're in for with this carefree approach. After all, there is no one else you'd rather be on a desert isle with than the one you're marrying. This invitation is a way to embody that idea.

DIRECTIONS FOR BOTTLE

1. Pour about ½ tablespoon of sand into the bottle. Add several tiny seashells, pieces of beach glass, crystal beads, or other beach findings to the bottle.

2. Glue the ¼" (2 cm) seashell to the top of the cork.

3. Construct the pull-cord for the invitation: Measure approximately 24" (61 cm) of turquoise embroidery floss. Using a flexible beading needle, thread beads on in the following order: 1 seashell, 1 small pearl, 1 medium blue bead, 3 tiny blue beads, 1 medium fish bead, 1 small crystal bead, 1 tiny turquoise bead, 1 small crystal bead, 1 tiny turquoise bead, 1 small crystal bead, 1 tiny turquoise bead, 1 medium blue bead, 1 small pearl bead, 1 seashell, 1 medium turquoise bead, 1 tiny turquoise bead.

4. At last bead, bring needle and floss through the hole in the tiny bead, then bring it around the outside of the tiny bead and back up through the medium turquoise bead.

5. Tie the floss off to the floss that is going down through the bead, pull, knot tie, and trim closely. Repeat beading process at other end of floss.

TIP *Make sure your shell sticker is large enough to hold all the layers together, otherwise the invitation may be difficult to pry from the mouth of the bottle.*

Catherine Smith

and

Anthony Renzi

invite you to share their joy

as they unite in marriage

and afterward for a clambake

and dancing in the sand

Saturday, September sixth

one o'clock in the afternoon

on the beach at Lighthouse Resort

Brigantine, New Jersey

Kindly rep

M

will

PROJECT DESIGN: ANDREA RENZI M^cFADDEN

MATERIALS FOR INVITATION

1 seashell sticker

paper and vellum in shades of pale blue and turquoise

mailing tube— 2" × 12" (5 cm × 30 cm)

bubble wrap

wave-pattern paper-edger scissors

double-sided tape

DIRECTIONS FOR INVITATION

1. Typeset then print your invitation on text weight paper (Don't use card stock, it will be too thick to roll tightly enough to fit in the bottle).

2. Print invitation landscape: Make two columns, center invitation in each column, or use best method for your computer so you can fit two on a page.

3. Trim to 5 ½" wide by 7" long (14 cm × 18 cm), using wave pattern craft scissors to trim bottom.

4. Cut a piece of turquoise vellum 5 ½" wide by 7 ¼" long (14 cm × 18.5 cm), using wave-pattern paper-edger scissors to trim bottom.

5. Cut a piece of pale blue vellum 5 ½" wide by 6 ¾" long (14 cm × 17.5 cm), and then use craft scissors with wave pattern to trim bottom off.

6. Stack the invitation, first turquoise vellum, then invitation, then pale vellum, so you can see the graduating wave pattern. Use double-sided tape at the top between the layers to hold together.

7. Lay the invitation out, printed side up. Place the pull cord across it, parallel with the side with the scalloped edge, so that about 5" (13 cm) hangs over one side of the invitation, and roll the invitation tightly enough for it to fit in the bottle. Use a seashell sticker to secure the invitation to itself. Take the long end of the pull cord and bring it over to meet the other end. Then place the invitation in the bottle with the beading hanging out. Put the cork in the bottle.

DIRECTIONS FOR RSVP

1. Print "RSVP" 5 ⅕" wide × 4" high (13.2 cm × 10 cm) in upper third of page.

2. Cut pale blue vellum 5 ½" wide × 1 ½" high (14 cm × 4 cm).

3. Cut turquoise vellum 5 ½" wide × 1 ¼" high (14 cm × 3.5 cm).

4. Trim the top of each piece of vellum with the wave-pattern paper-edger scissors. Attach the pale blue then the turquoise vellum to the bottom portion of the RSVP card with double-sided tape. Put one or more seashell stickers on the reply envelope for decoration.

5. Wrap your RSVP around the bottle, wrap with a layer of bubble wrap, and put in mailing tube for shipping.

VARIATION *Place some other fun small items in the bottle, like a pair of miniature flip-flops, sunglasses or bride-and-groom cupcake decorations.*

MATERIALS FOR RSVP

card stock

turquoise vellum

pale blue vellum

5 ½" × 4" (14 cm × 10 cm) envelope

wave-pattern paper-edger scissors

seashell stickers

double-sided tape

marriage

i do

joy

passion

pebble beach country club

party

pebble beach, california.

family

henning thormaelen

forever

lynne g. waring

groom

happiness

march 3, 2004

bride

friends

2 p.m. in the afternoon

love

50

Magnetic Couple
POETRY KIT

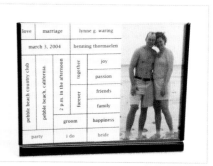

Is your love a poem that is rewritten every day? Do your feelings for each other run so deep you're weak in the knees and your thoughts are a jumble? No matter how you rearrange these words, they spell out one thing: great, witty wedding ahead. The pop culture reference that this invitation is based on begs people to play well before they even arrive at the big shindig. Find your guests' not-so-inner Shakespeare. Include instructions, if you think friends won't get the idea right off the bat (your Great-Aunt Hazel might have missed the magnetic poetry craze, after all).

DIRECTIONS

1. In your page layout program, create a new document 11" wide × 8 ½" deep (28 cm × 22 cm).

2. Create a box 5" wide × 3 ½" deep (13 cm × 9 cm).

3. Place digital bride-and-groom photo in page on the right side of the box (ours measures 2" wide × 3 ½" tall (5 cm × 9 cm)).

4. In the same 5" wide × 3 ½" tall (13 cm × 9 cm) box, set type for invitation, dividing words with black rules (we used 9 point Lucida Fax type). Set some of the type horizontally and some vertically to make it look like a game board (see photo above right).

5. Once you've decided on a grid and design you like, copy the box and its graphic elements three times. Set them up on the page 2 across and 2 down.

6. Print out onto an 8 ½" × 11" (22 cm × 28 cm) Avery (or comparable brand) magnet sheet and trim exterior edges.

7. Place onto steel board (optional).

TIP *Create a "How to Play the Game" instruction booklet for the guests. Tell them to cut out the invitation words and place them on their refrigerator doors or the steel game board.*

MATERIALS

digitized photo of the bride and groom

8 ½" × 11" (22 cm × 28 cm) Avery magnet sheets

personal computer

scanner

color printer

page layout software (such as Quark or PageMaker)

metal ruler

craft knife

4" × 6" (10 cm × 15 cm) steel board (optional)

Swatch Us Get Hitched
PANTONE-STYLE INVITE

This invitation is based on the Pantone swatch booklets that designers use. Some people may not recognize it, but that doesn't diminish the intrigue of the off-center-pivoting, elongated invite. Sleek and contained within the envelope, it splays out to show all of the information needed for the event. Print cover on glossy photo paper and the inside on thick matte photo paper.

DIRECTIONS

1. In your page layout software, create a series of text boxes that each measure 2 ⅛ " wide × 7 ⅝" tall (6 cm × 19.5 cm).

2. Scan the images from page 292, or find some suitable clip art images. Import them into the documents and center each one at the top of the corresponding text boxes.

3. Write the invitation, directions, and reception information. (We used ACaslon Regular Small Caps for the font.) For the cover, pivot the text so it runs along the long edge. Leave plenty of room at the bottom so the text does not run too close to the screw post. We wrote "weddings" in a sans serif font to mimic the style of the booklet that inspired this invitation. We also added the year "04" in the space where the trademark usually sits.

4. Print the cover on glossy photo paper. Print the inserts on a thick matte photo paper. Trim to size. Round the corners with a corner punch.

5. Punch a hole in the lower left corner, ¼" (.5 cm) from the edges. If your hole punch is too large for the screw post shaft, use a star-shaped punch and some of the interior corners will provide friction.

TIP *Make sure that the paper fills the length of the screw post shaft. If the paper you have chosen is too thin to fill up the length of the shaft, you can use an eyelet in place of the screw post. You can then thread a key ring through the eyelet and add a charm.*

MATERIALS

personal computer

scanner

color printer

page layout software (such as Quark or PageMaker)

images (see the templates on page 292)

scissors

ruler

hole punch

curvy corner punch

short nickel-plated screw posts

glossy photo paper

thick matte photo paper

Cork Popper

CHAMPAGNE BOTTLE LABEL

MATERIALS

personal computer

page layout
software
(such as Quark
or PageMaker)

color printer

colored paper

paper trimmer

PVA glue,
neutral adhesive,
or Fast Tack

Granted, if you are inviting hundreds of people to your wedding, the postage for this invite alone would be formidable. Let's be fair, this may not faze you at all, or it may leave you sitting with your head between your knees. However, for a smaller wedding, or one that is focused on a certain feeling (think tuxedos, New Year's Eve, and decadence), sometimes a little extra hits the mood just right. Buy half-bottles of your favorite champagne (see, we're showing a little restraint) and cover the labels with an invitation. Leave the real label intact underneath so people can know what they're drinking as they toast your impending nuptials (because that's the idea with this kind of an invitation). We mimicked the border treatment of the real label, and printed the invitation on a paper that matched the label.

DIRECTIONS

1. Measure the label on the bottle. Create a text box on your computer that measures $1/4$" (0.5 cm) larger in both dimensions. Set the invitation wording in the text box.

2. Print the invitation on the paper. Trim to size. We used vellum on our invitation and glued two layers together to achieve the proper opacity. If you are using a regular paper, you will probably not need to layer the paper.

3. Make sure the surface of the bottle is clean and free from grease. Run a thin bead of glue around the edges of the invitation and carefully center on the bottle label. Smooth the invitation onto the bottle and hold in place for a few second to let the glue set.

TIP *Check mailing laws for the states and countries you will be mailing to. Buy some sparking cider or other non-alcoholic beverage for those places that will not accept alcohol—or to send to those friends who don't drink the hard stuff.*

MILLE SEPT CENT
SOIXANTE DOUZE

TOGETHER WITH THE HOWARDS AND THE BERTRANDS

GWENDOLYN HAZEL HOWARD
AND
ALAN NICHOLAS BERTRAND

INVITE YOU TO JOIN THEM
AT THEIR WEDDING
DECEMBER THIRTY-FIRST, NEW YEAR'S EVE
AT EIGHT O'CLOCK
SAINT IGNACIO, CHICAGO, ILLINOIS

PLEASE CELEBRATE WITH THEM AFTERWARD
AS THEY RAISE A GLASS AND TOAST
THEIR FUTURE, THEIR FRIENDS, AND THE NEW YEAR
AT THE PALMER HOUSE

Longevity

ESSENTIAL FOR MARRIAGE BUT NOT FOR INVITATIONS

When you buy a black dress or sling-back shoes, you may consider how classic the design is. If that dress has a little Audrey Hepburn to it, you are pleased that the style will endure and that you will get years of use from its classic form. If you buy an expensive suit, you consider how wearable it will be five years down the line. That's a smart way to think—when you are dealing with items you will use repeatedly.

Your invitation is one-time-use only. Sure, you may keep it tucked away someplace safe and reminisce about the wedding day when you uncover it. Your friends, however, probably do not have such long-term plans for the invitation, no matter how much thought you put into it. Your best bet is to treat an invitation like a piece of performance art rather than a gallery piece. It will fulfill its duty and be done.

There's no need to be shackled to a classic design just because it will withstand the test of time. If you and your sweetheart want something a little witty, goofy, or out of the ordinary, don't fret about how it will look in twenty years. You are meant for the next twenty years, but your invitations are good only until the main event. And so what if someone keeps the invitation and occasionally rags you about how your style was so 2004? Quel compliment! Now that is impact.

Likewise, it's no reason to chuck convention out the window if that fits your style the best. You don't have to take advantage of an invitation's short tenure just because you can—only do so if it suits you.

The same style sense that tells you which clothes to buy will also inform your choice of invitation, but you are no doubt able to take that style to a more outlandish point, if that's your desire. There's no point in choosing a sedate invitation for fear of how it will look in twenty years. If you stick to your sense of self, style, and personality, you won't have any trouble.

If you *are* thinking down the long line, consider how fantastic your style is already, and how it is supposed to change over time. Don't believe us? Go to your closet. Way in the back. See those outfits you couldn't possibly give away, but couldn't bear to wear? They were perfect once, but they wouldn't do you any favors now. But you still love them for how perfectly they suited you then. Same goes for invitation and wedding decisions. We can't always please who we will be decades from now, but we will have a better chance of wonderful memories if we relax and live it up now. Longevity may be the goal of a marriage, but don't eschew the delights of the temporal when planning the invitation style and wedding details. People would much rather see your excitement and style bursting through an invitation that may not suit you in a few years than receive something that says nothing about you and your intended.

What to Say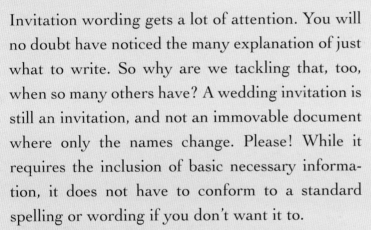

GETTING THE WORDS RIGHT

Invitation wording gets a lot of attention. You will no doubt have noticed the many explanation of just what to write. So why are we tackling that, too, when so many others have? A wedding invitation is still an invitation, and not an immovable document where only the names change. Please! While it requires the inclusion of basic necessary information, it does not have to conform to a standard spelling or wording if you don't want it to.

Etiquette books make a good read. They are almost like novels in their fascinating twists and situations. They are reliable, but not infallible, and there is no reason to shun their advice out of some misguided inclination that etiquette is boorish. Proper etiquette is not snobbery. We turn to these books to learn how to put people at ease, make a graceful expression, and treat people with respect. That makes sense. We know some people who read them for sheer curiosity (okay, okay, guilty!). After all, you might run into the Dalai Lama or a Supreme Court justice, and you'll enjoy the encounter all the more if you know how to greet them in a way that is familiar and comfortable for them. (For that matter, you want to know how to make proper introductions or seat people at a party for maximum enjoyment.) However, following style books to the letter disallows your own graceful creativity. Keep in mind that they are called "guides," not "rule books." They are meant to help you wade through waters you might be nervous about; they are not meant to make you an unwilling manners puppet.

There are several books that will provide you with elaborate explanations of wedding invitation wording. Not all of the guidance will agree. That's okay, because that's what personal style is for, baby! *Here are the basics:*

1. Include the who, what, where, when, and any "how" that might be necessary, such as "ice skating to follow" or "summer hats welcome."

2. Traditional wording and spelling includes requesting the "honour" of someone's presence with the time and date spelled out completely.

3. An invitation is issued by the hosts. That's why many invitations start off with the names of the bride's parents: "Mr. and Mrs. Philippe Hughes are thrilled to invite you to the marriage of their daughter . . . ." More and more couples are hosting their own weddings, however, so the wording can come directly from the couple: "Our joy will be more complete if you join with us, Marjorie Allen and Trevor LaTourelle, in our marriage on . . . ."

4. The year is not necessary in an invitation, because the date is in the near future.

We got hitched!
Tim & Kim Gray
3.15.2003

A Thousand Words
GIGANTIC PHOTO SLIDE

Let people in on a moment from your honeymoon with a giant photo slide. Instead of showing people an entire slideshow of your trip, this card pokes a little fun at that (dare we say boring?) tradition. This card works as a thank-you note and shares with recipients a little about where you went and some of what you did. It also works brilliantly as an announcement that you eloped. Subtly funny, the slide offers a retro-style way to share your memories with people you love.

DIRECTIONS FOR SLIDE

1. Create a new document in your page layout program 4 ¾" (11.5 cm) square.

2. Create a 3 ½" wide × 3" deep (9 cm × 8 cm) picture box and import the photograph into your document from your compact disc. Leave about 1" (3 cm) on the bottom for your type and center the picture box left and right in your document.

3. Size picture to fit box.

4. Add your personalized text to the bottom of the page as shown in the photo.

5. Print the document onto transparency film at 104 percent.

6. Trim newly created transparency slide with craft knife, leaving about ¼" (0.5 cm) around outside edge of image area.

7. Load printer with a sheet of card stock and output two copies of the document, this time at 100 percent.

8. Cut both copies out and die-cut the corners with the rounded corner punch.

VARIATION *Insert one of these slides into an envelope with a thank-you card. Make the thank-you card the same proportions and use the corner punch to mirror the giant slide.*

MATERIALS

photo from your honeymoon on a compact disc

8 ½" × 11" (22 cm × 28 cm) inkjet or laser transparency film (to match your printer)

8 ½" × 11" (22 cm × 28 cm) inkjet or laser card stock

personal computer

page layout software (such as Quark or PageMaker)

color printer

craft knife

metal ruler

pencil

rounded corner punch

glue stick

snazzybags.com silver envelope 5" × 7 ¾" (13 cm × 20 cm)

fig. 1

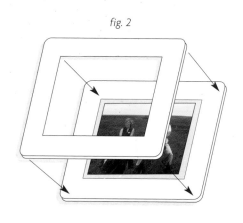

9. Cut out center windows on both copies. You have just created the frame for the slide.

10. Center, then adhere transparency to back of frame with glue stick *(see fig. 1)*.

11. Center, then adhere back of frame to front of frame with glue stick *(see fig. 2)*.

DIRECTIONS FOR SLIDE EASEL

1. Photocopy the easel template from page 293 and cut out the photocopy.

2. Place a piece of the card stock on your work surface. Place template over card stock and trace around outside edges. Cut out newly created card-stock easel.

3. Fold, then glue tab to back of card *(see fig. 3)*.

4. Place in silver envelope.

5. Create mailing labels for the outside envelope using a mailing label system, such as Avery, or handwrite them yourself onto an adhesive-backed label.

fig. 2

fig. 3

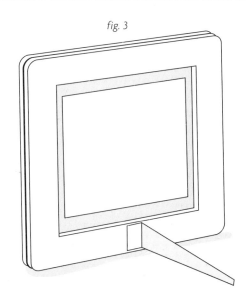

We got hitched!
Tim & Kim Gray
3 . 15 . 2003

Refrigerator Reminder

MAGNETIC SAVE-THE-DATE CARD

What good is a save-the-date card if you can never find it? Losing things (pieces of paper, say) doesn't necessarily make you disorganized. There is just so much to keep track of sometimes that even the happiest bits of mail get buried. It happens to the best of us, including your nearest and dearest. Give your guests half a chance. This card is magnetic and will make a stylish and functional addition to the fridge door. Along with the message, the wedding date is circled on a small calendar, making it an extra-effective reminder.

DIRECTIONS

1. Create an 8 ½" × 11" document in your page layout program.

2. Draw a rectangle 4" wide × 6" deep (10 cm × 15 cm) on the page.

3. Scan icon, save as a .tiff file, and place on page.

4. Color icon maroon.

5. Create stripes of varying thickness in background and color them lime green, orange, and pink.

6. Set type for reminder.

7. Duplicate the card and place it next to the other one, so you can print two up at a time (see fig. 1).

8. Print onto card stock or glossy photo paper.

9. Trim and place in plexiglass frame.

10. Wrap in pink tissue and place in envelope.

VARIATION *Thanks to adhesive magnet sheets, you can make a true magnet out of your paper card. Simply print the card, peel back the magnetic sheet's protective paper, and press the card onto the magnet sheet, smoothing any air bubbles away with a bone folder.*

MATERIALS

4" wide × 6" deep (10 cm × 15 cm) plexiglass frame with magnet on back

personal computer

scanner

color printer

page layout software (such as Quark or PageMaker)

8 ½" × 11" (22 cm × 28 cm) laser or inkjet card stock or glossy photo paper

4 ¼" × 6 ½" (10.5 cm × 17 cm) lime green vellum envelope

clip art of wedding location or representative icon

pink tissue paper

Tea and Camaraderie
TEA PARTY INVITATION

MATERIALS

personal computer

scanner

color printer

page layout software
(such as Quark
or PageMaker)

templates from
page 292

8 ½" × 11"
(22 cm × 28 cm)
cream-colored laser
or inkjet card stock

craft knife

metal ruler

bone folder

glue stick

tea bag

stapler

scissors

5 ¾" (14.5 cm)
square light
blue envelope

Showers come in many forms, from strobe-light-accompanied nights on the town to comparatively sedate get-togethers where friends can chat or catch up on the latest. A tea party is a perfect example of the latter. Tea, sandwiches, cookies, and—best of all—a chance to hang out with your pals. This invitation sums it up with a hands-on icon. The style is reminiscent of dreamy Italian moderne posters and gives the clear hint that the tea party won't be a trip into a world of ultraproper, pinky-raising tea sipping. And don't forget, more and more showers are for the couple, instead of just the bride. This invitation has enough of a masculine edge to suit a couple's shower as well.

DIRECTIONS

1. Create an 11" wide × 8 ½" deep (28 cm × 22 cm) document in your page layout program.

2. Scan in template from page 292 at 200 percent and save as an eps file. Place eps in your document.

3. On back panel of the placed template, typeset the words for the invitation.

4. Print out invitation from your color printer onto the cream-colored card stock.

5. Using your craft knife and metal ruler, cut out the invitation.

6. Cut slit in teacup following black line provided in template.

7. Lightly score fold areas lightly with craft knife and ruler *(see fig. 1 on page 66).*

TIP *Use a nice tea bag for this invitation. Go to the store and buy a couple of tea varieties (you can drink them, after all) in your quest to find a nice-looking tea bag with a nice tag. You may already drink a variety that fits the design perfectly (we like Twinings), but if not, do a little research for optimal impact.*

8. Fold in flap edges *(see fig. 2)* and burnish with the bone folder.

9. Glue flap edges with glue stick and adhere front to back panels *(see fig. 3)*.

10. Scan "you're invited" tea tag from page 292 in at 100 percent, then print and cut out.

11. Cut off the existing tag from a tea bag and staple "you're invited" tag to the tea bag string, tying off a knot around the staple, leaving 3" (8 cm) of string hanging from tea bag to tea tag.

12. Trim end of string with scissors and place tea bag into card.

13. Fill out card and place into blue envelope.

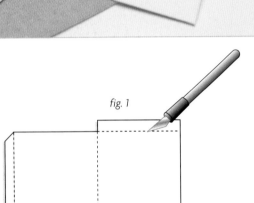

fig. 1

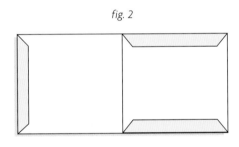

fig. 2

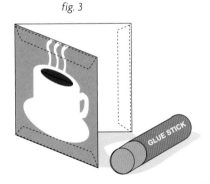

fig. 3

Please join us for a
Bridal Shower & Tea

honoring
Lynne Waring

Sunday, January 18, 2004
at eleven a.m.

100 Lake Point
Swansea, Mass.

PLEASE R.S.V.P. TO KARINA BY JANUARY 5
(401) 299-3434

Lynne's
Peppermint
Herbal Tea

VARIATION *For a different look, you can make your own tea wrapper,
with requisite invitation information placed directly on the packaging.*

Where in the World?

DESTINATION INVITATION

Destination weddings are increasingly popular. And for good reason — they're a blast. Everyone is from out of town and ready for adventure. And what an adventure a wedding is to begin with. Why not go the extra step and involve Rio, Hawaii, or Tuscany? Point guests to the destination with these travel-themed "luggage tags." The mounting excitement of a trip to take part in a friend's wedding is enhanced by the brightly colored tags and retro luxury liner logos.

DIRECTIONS FOR FRONT OF INVITATION

1. Create a 4 ½" wide × 4" deep (11 cm × 10 cm) document in your page layout program.

2. Scan or find website of appropriate map and place it into your page layout program. Set the type "You are here" in white and place over an arrow dingbat (in this case, we used a Zapf Dingbat.) Color the arrow red so it is very visible.

3. Print out the map onto an 8 ½" × 11" (22 cm × 28 cm) sheet of label paper and trim it to size with deckled-edge scissors or rotary paper trimmer (outfitted with the deckled-edged blade).

4. Place 4 ½" × 6" (11 cm × 15 cm) tag on work surface, grommet facing left. Center map label on rectangular area of tag and adhere.

DIRECTIONS FOR BACK OF INVITATION

1. Color photocopy or scan the larger ticket template from page 293 and place onto 8 ½" × 11" (22 cm × 28 cm) adhesive label paper.

2. Trim to size with craft knife and ruler (or rotary trimmer with straight edge blade) and place on back of 4 ½" × 6" (11 cm × 15 cm) tag.

3. Loop cording through tag hole, knot, and trim ends.

4. Handwrite card with appropriate information and place in large envelope.

DIRECTIONS FOR RSVP

1. Color photocopy or scan the smaller ticket template from page 293 and place onto an 8 ½" × 11" (22 cm × 28 cm) adhesive label paper.

2. Trim to size.

3. Adhere to smaller red hang tag.

4. Loop cording through tag hole, knot, and trim ends.

5. Place in smaller envelope.

TIP *You can substitute a street map of the wedding location instead of the country map.*

flip your calendar
and save-the-date

PROJECT DESIGN: CHRISTINE TRAULICH, WWW.REDBLISS.COM

Flip-Flop Plan

BEACH-Y SAVE-THE-DATE CARD

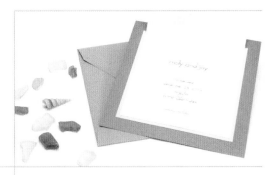

Few things say summer and beach time like a bright pair of flip-flops. The breezy—and delightfully kitchy—attitude that this save-the-date card conveys reflects the casual and vibrant atmosphere you will no doubt achieve at your wedding festivities. Think drinks with little umbrellas, think fire-dancing luau performers, think clam-bake rehearsal dinner, think the ultimate in beach fun. With a card that is elegant in its humorous references, guests will be prepared to be a little windswept and sandblown as they attend the joining of equal, carefree minds in a ceremony by the sea. Flip-flops are the footwear of the playful and at-ease types, so opt for a different icon if you are looking for ultimate seaside refinement.

DIRECTIONS

1. Cut Neutron blue cardstock into 5 ½" (14 cm) squares.

2. Cut yellow Razzle cardstock into 4 ½" (11 cm) squares.

3. Cut white Cryogen fold over cards down to 4 ½" (11 cm) squares.

4. Create a document 4 ½" wide × 8 ½" deep (11 cm × 22 cm) in your favorite page layout program. Set text for the front and inside of the save-the-date card and colorize text blue.

5. Print front and inside of card onto the white Cryogen fold-over cards.

6. Assemble and spray adhere the layers in the following order: Neutron blue (bottom), yellow Razzle (middle), white Cryogren (top).

7. Adhere flip-flops to the top of the fold-over card.

8. Place card in envelope.

VARIATION *Choose an icon from nature to convey a quieter, coastal to-do. Use a small starfish, sand dollar, or scallop shell, and guests will anticipate a more sedate, pristine, and refined occasion.*

MATERIALS

8 ½" × 11" (22 cm × 28 cm) blue Neutron card stock

8 ½" × 11" (22 cm × 28 cm) yellow Razzle card stock

A2 white Cryogen fold-over cards

5 ¼" (14.5 cm) blue envelopes

1" (3 cm) foam flip-flops

color printer

page layout program (such as Quark or PageMaker)

paper cutter or craft knife and ruler

spray adhesive

We Eloped!

POST-GETAWAY ANNOUNCEMENT

MATERIALS

8 ½" × 14"
(22 cm × 36 cm)
white laser or inkjet
card stock

postage stamp from
wedding destination

inking stamp from
wedding destination

inkpad with brown ink

jpeg honeymoon photo

personal computer

page layout software
(such as Quark
or PageMaker)

photo manipulation
software (such as
Photoshop)

scanner

color printer

5 ¾" (14.5 cm)
square pale
green envelope

photo corners

bone folder

craft knife

glue stick

Think that escaping for a matrimonial getaway leaves you craftless? Think again! Any invitation listed in this book can be adapted to create a stunning announcement of your nouveau marital status. This announcement, however, is specially designed for those of you who do not want to go through the full-on wedding planning. No matter how you usher in your marriage, share the joy and a glimpse into your sneak attack on wedded bliss.

DIRECTIONS

1. Scan postage stamp into your computer at about 200 percent. Save as an .eps file.

2. Import image into Photoshop or equivalent program.

3. Set the type in Photoshop and colorize.

4. Rotate the photo 7 degrees clockwise.

5. Create a new document in your page layout program 4" (10 cm) square.

6. Place the stamp .eps into the center of the document, and scale it up until it measures 2 ½" (6 cm) wide.

7. Trim document to size.

8. Create a separate document in your page layout program 4" deep × 12" wide (10 cm × 30 cm). Divide into three equal sections making the first section pale blue, the second one olive green, and the third one pale blue.

9. Place photo corners around a photo of you and your spouse and scan as a tiff file.

VARIATION *If you don't have a stamp from your destination, consider using a tacky postcard or souvenir. Forgot to get one? (We know, you were busy.) Check out eBay or your favorite "kitsch" shop if your destination is culturally popular, like Hawaii or the Caribbean.*

10. Import image into the the first blue panel of your document and scale until it is 3" (8 cm) wide. Center on page.

11. Type message in panel 2.

12. Print and then trim to size.

13. Stamp with inking stamp from destination on panel 3.

14. Fold and score at color breaks with bone folder so it makes a Z-fold with three separate sections.

15. Glue stick the front cover and burnish it to back side of the first panel of the Z-fold.

16. Stamp exterior envelope with destination ink stamp on front and back.

How Many Prizes Are Inside?

THE ELEMENTS OF AN INVITATION

Strictly speaking, any invitation should contain only an invitation, a reply card, and a stamped envelope for the reply card. All three elements should be contained in the main envelope. Directions and other information should be sent separately after the response is received.

Tradition has dictated that formal invitations be sent in a double envelope. That means that the outer envelope that is marked up and dirtied by its trip through the postal system is opened to reveal a pristine envelope that contains the invitation and reply materials. This double envelope harkens back to the days when footmen delivered messages by hand. The outer envelope was susceptible to flecks of mud from the dirt street, finger prints, footprints, you name it. The outer envelope was discarded at the recipient's house, revealing an impeccable envelope with only the intended person's name on it (after all, the footman had delivered it to the proper address, so the house number was no longer needed). That style of packaging has remained somehow. Although it's unlikely that a clod of dirt will be chucked up from a passing horse cart onto the invitation envelope, the pure and clean interior envelope is like a drum roll. You know you are about to open something important. It's exciting! Today, that inside envelope still has only the names of the recipients on it, with no address. Essentially, the postal service is acting as an automated and expert footman. It's a cleaner process all round these days, so don't feel wedded to the double enclosure if you think it's over the top.

That amounts to five pieces of paper: the outer envelope, the inner envelope, the invitation, the reply card, and the envelope for the reply card. And yet, most of the invitations we've received over the years have been packed tighter than a sausage with maps, directions, messages, cards to fill with memories, lists of hotels, and so on. Including these pieces assures that you won't forget to send it later. But there is a trade-off to consider fully before making that choice. Packing the invitation with all the extras draws a lot of attention away from the invitation. The double envelope sets the stage for an impact, but the gorgeous invitation you made may easily be lost in a world of photocopied maps or hotel lists.

There are some things you can do to keep the focus on the invite:

- Prepare a second mailing with all of the extra information. Send it immediately after the invitation, or wait until you receive people's responses.
- Don't use photocopies. The full-size sheet is often folded into thick quarters and shoved into the envelope, taking up room and hiding the more beautiful elements. The ink from the photocopy flakes off along the folds.
- If you would like to include the extras with the invitation, scan any images or maps into the computer. Type messages to accompany them and keep the size down. Make the info documents twice the size of the invitation (at the most) and fold them cleanly in half so they fit easily into the envelope. Do not print anything on the fold line.

- Incorporate the invitation additions into the invitation design. Instead of making them seem like an add-on, make them belong.
- Use a large enough envelope. If you are putting a lot of items into an envelope, make it easy and smooth, not a demonstration in cramming and paper cuts. When in doubt, choose an envelope that's a bit larger and make it easier for your guests to slide out your invitation.

Invitation stuffing may not be ideal, but it may be the best choice for you. Consider how to make the information succinct and effective, as well as unobtrusive. Simple information always trumps a novella in this case. And if you're adding things in, don't forget that your add-ins can go beyond the usual information. You could add a card into the invitations of people with kids encouraging them to bring their lovely offspring—and a change of clothes for the afternoon of games. You could include an invitation to a brunch the next morning, as that might affect some people's early-made travel plans. Dream it up, but keep it to the point and small. And if you can resist, let the invitation do its job before showering people with all the minor details.

THE CALLIGRAPHIC WEDDING

You've dreamed about this day your entire life. And as you move further and further into the planning process of your wedding, each and every detail seems to grow in importance. Small elements combine to create a full-bodied effect.

The written word has great prominence in wedding festivities. It may be in an obvious capacity, such as invitations, place cards, or menus. Or it may be something less noticeable, such as a favor tag, the name on a guest book, or a handwritten note on a gift basket sent to a guest's hotel room. The opportunities for beautiful lettering are vast. Calligraphy can enhance your writing at its core.

This chapter provides a basic introduction to calligraphy and some of the multitudes of lettering styles—some simple, others more complex. With a little thought or with minor changes, your alphabet of choice can be translated to any project in the chapter. Calligraphy is versatile and transcends any classifications we impose upon it.

The projects in this chapter incorporate a full range of wedding concerns, from engagement to postwedding activities. Invitations, envelopes, and place cards are the most obvious items with which calligraphy is typically used. There are also ideas for gift tags, guest books to record good wishes, programs, and more. The quality of your finished product will be affected by the quality of your materials, so choose fine papers, ribbons, and flowers for these projects, and you won't be disappointed.

Practice, relax, and enjoy the learning process. Above all, let your own character, your own vision, and your own penmanship shine on the page. Don't strive for perfection; strive for personality.

I am my beloved's and my beloved is mine.

SONG OF SOLOMON 6:3

Jennifer and Michael
February 24, 2001

CLASSIC

Anna Marie Lacroix
and
Ramone Miguel Perez
invite you to celebrate their engagement
Friday, the tenth of August
at seven o'clock in the evening

The Beaumont
One Chanterelle Circle

I am my beloved's and
my beloved is mine.
SONG OF SOLOMON 6:3

Jennifer and Michael
February 24, 2001

FOR YOU

classic CALLIGRAPHY

Long before the printing press was invented, learned scribes spent countless hours studying the art of hand lettering. Only after years of practice would they be entrusted with preserving the words of scholars in the form of exquisite handwritten manuscripts. Successive civilizations developed new styles of lettering, building on their predecessors' artistry to suit a new function or aesthetic style.

Adapted to our modern alphabet, classic-style letterforms conjure up a sense of history, formality, and even sanctity. The alphabets presented in this chapter are stately, evoking feelings of reverence—perfect for the formality of a wedding. All use a broad pen nib to create the traditional letter shapes. The beginner may find it easier to start out with a broad-tipped calligraphy marker or a fountain pen. As you gain experience and confidence, draw inspiration from history and add picture blocks, colored borders, and letters that are enlarged and embellished to turn your wedding invitation into a timeless illuminated manuscript.

CALLIGRAPHER MELISSA DINWIDDIE

The Italic alphabet is one of the most commonly used for wedding calligraphy. A descendant of earlier, more laborious lettering styles, it became popular because it was relatively quick, requiring fewer lifts of the pen. To write in Italic script, a broad-edged pen is held at an angle between 35 and 45 degrees. The letters naturally slant toward the right with the pen angle. CALLIGRAPHER HILARY WILLIAMS

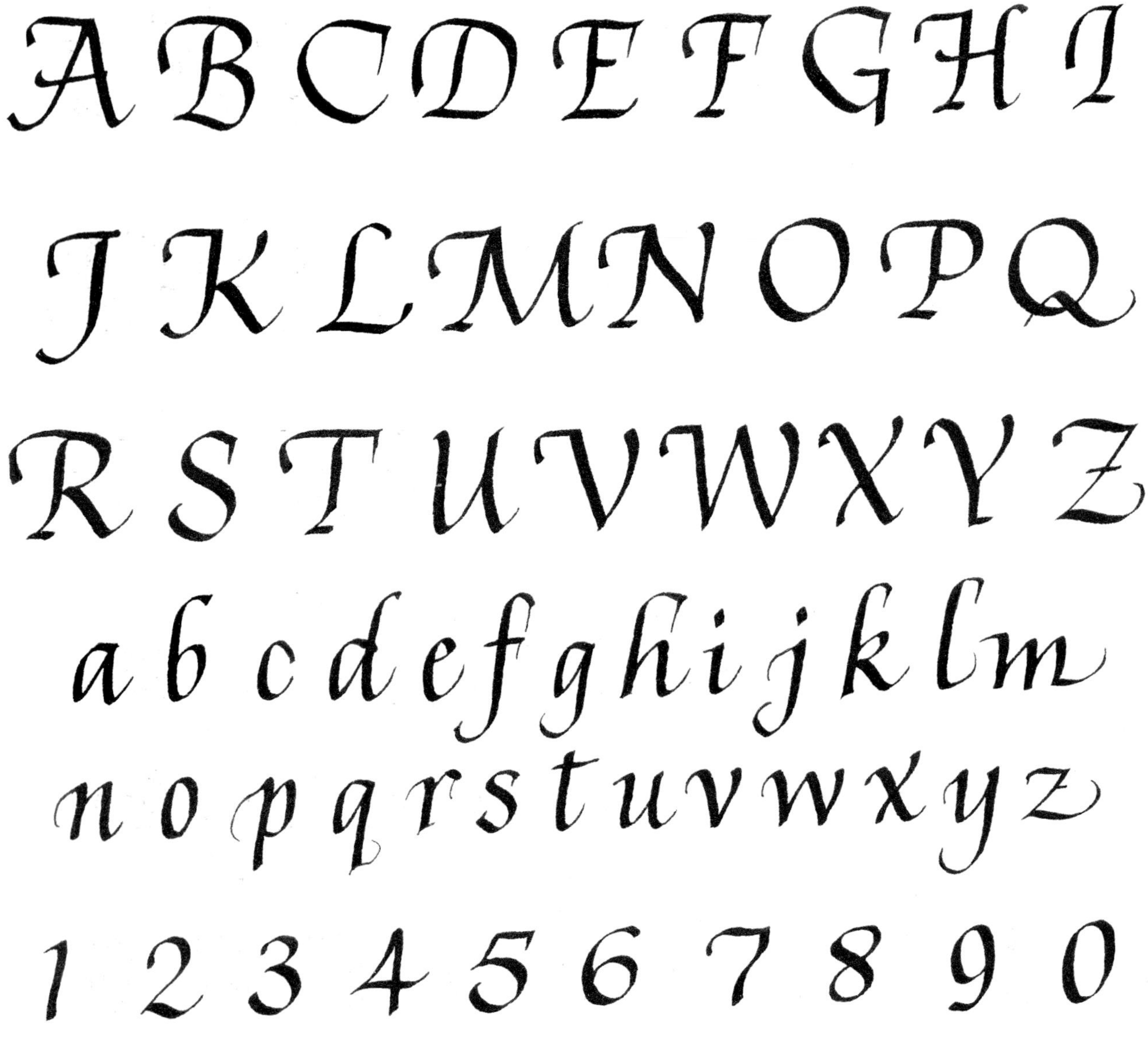

A B C D E F G H I
J K L M N O P Q
R S T U V W X Y Z
a b c d e f g h i j k l m
n o p q r s t u v w x y z
1 2 3 4 5 6 7 8 9 0

A B C D E F G H I
J K L M N O P Q
R S T U V W X Y Z
a b c d e f g h i j k l m
n o p q r s t u v w x y z
1 2 3 4 5 6 7 8 9 0

Uncial scripts, which date back to early Greek and Roman times, perfectly express the theme of a classic, modern-day wedding. The name "Uncial" (sounds like uhn-shul) means "inch" and was probably coined in reference to the large size of the lettering used in the decorative luxury books of the time. Many of our lowercase letters originate from this alphabet, and it is a good practice hand for beginners. CALLIGRAPHER MELISSA DINWIDDIE

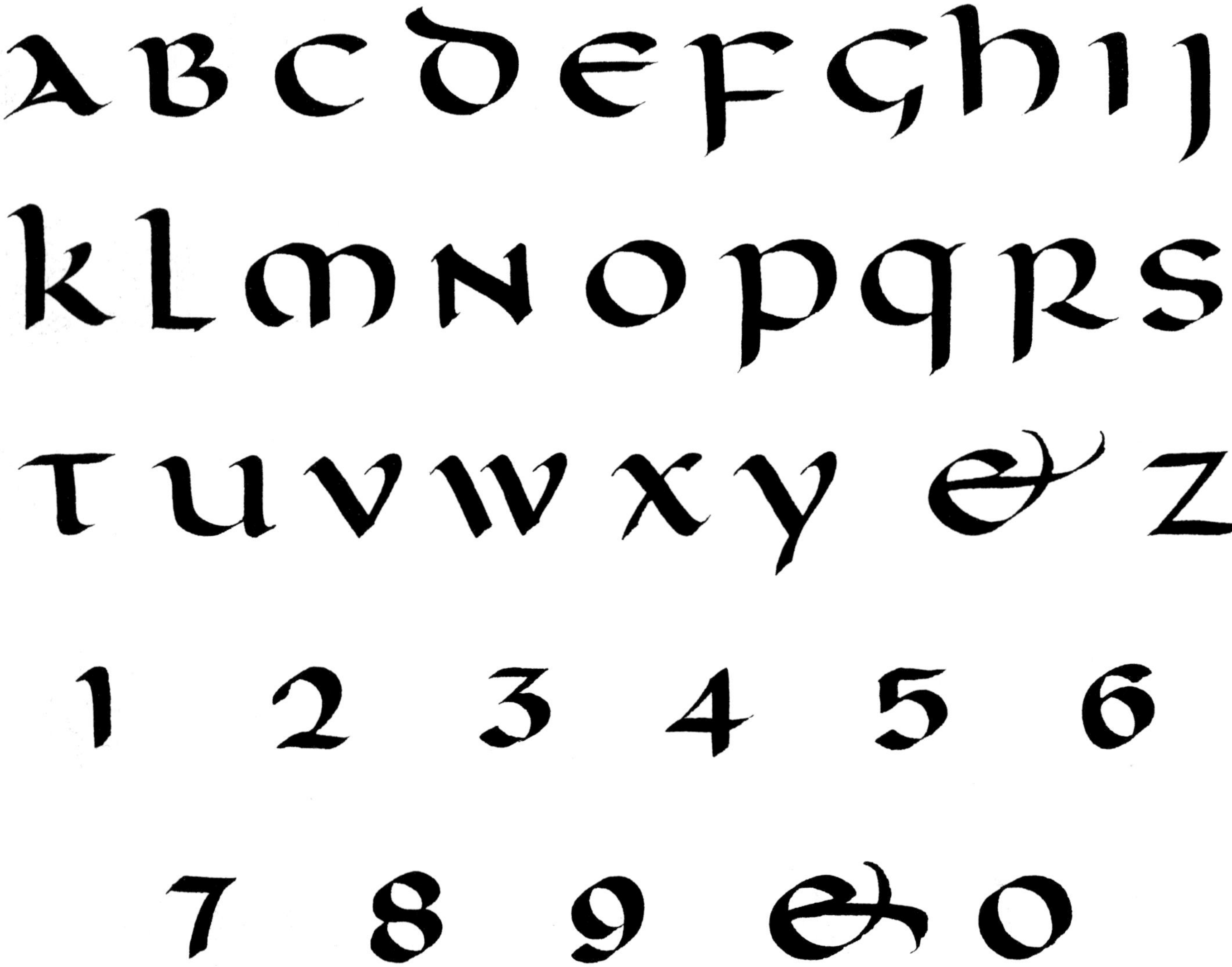

ABCDEFGhIJ

KLMNOPQRS

TUVWXY&Z

1 2 3 4 5 6

7 8 9 & 0

ABCDEFGHIJ

KLMNOPQRS

TUVWXY&Z

1 2 3 4 5 6

7 8 9 &O

Blackletter, Textura Quadrata, and Old English are common names for this lettering style. A descendant of an early Gothic alphabet, the letters are notably angular and upright, appropriate for announcing a more formal event. Ancient scribes seemed more concerned with the script's overall graphic effect than with its readability. This version of the letterform recognizes the importance of maintaining legibility without losing the formality of the alphabet. CALLIGRAPHER MELISSA DINWIDDIE

A B C D E F G H
I J K L M N O P Q
R S T U V W X Y Z
a b c d e f g h i j k l m
n o p q r s t u v w x y z
1 2 3 4 5 6 7 8 9 0

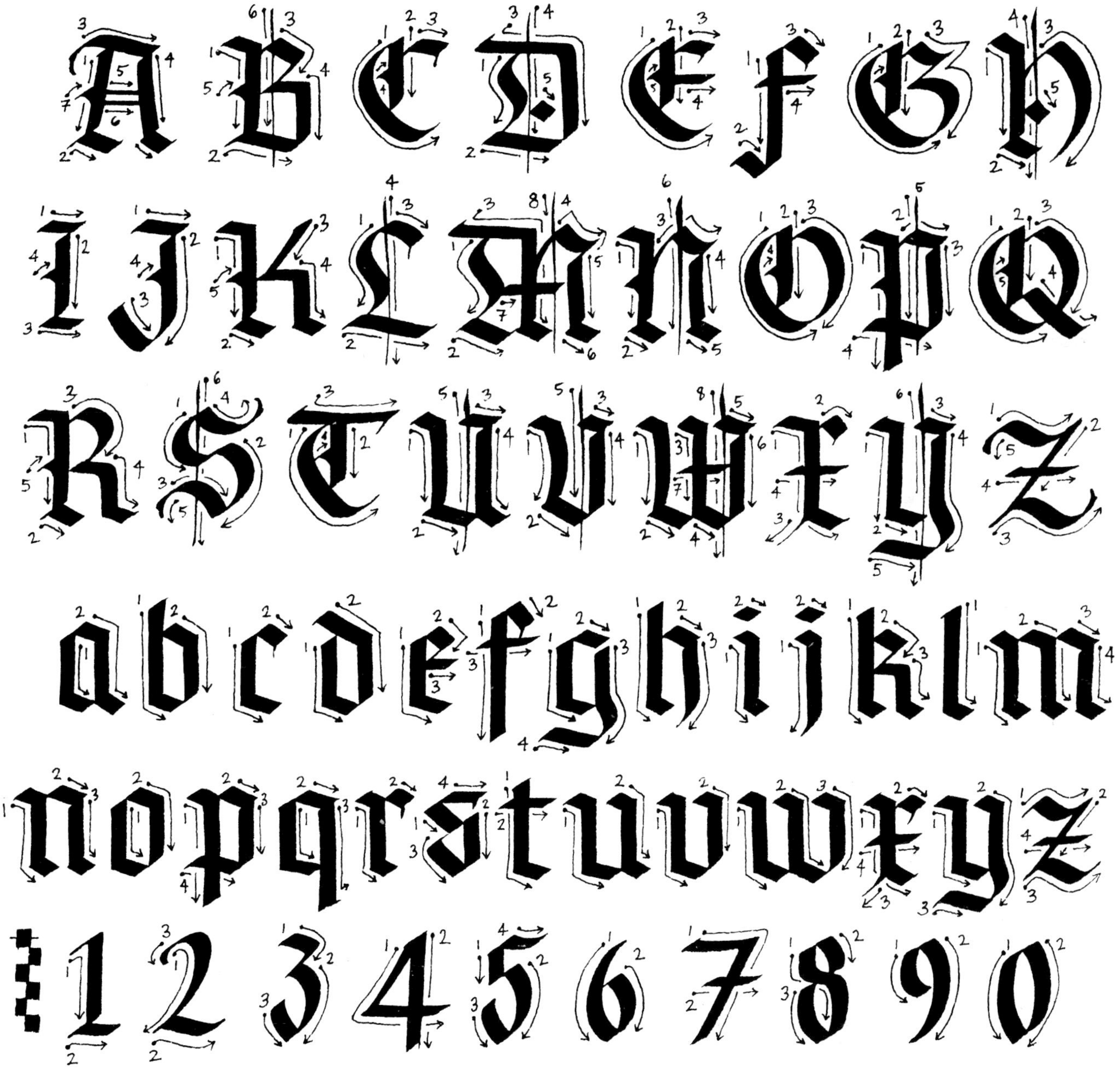

v e l l u m PLACE CARDS

Place cards let your guests know where to sit at the reception and present a perfect opportunity for using calligraphy at your wedding. This simple project is ideal for the beginner calligrapher. Variations on this project are also limitless for more experienced calligraphers. Cut the work in half by purchasing precut and prescored place cards at your local stationer or craft store. Vellum is a beautiful and forgiving paper choice for placing over your inscribed card. The translucent paper can jazz up a plain card or soften a lively design while masking slight imperfections. Vellum comes in various shades, colors, and patterns. Try a patterned card underneath a solid colored vellum, or experiment with colored inks and flourishes to match the vellum pattern.

MATERIALS

- purchased place cards made from lightweight card stock
- calligraphy fountain pen
- black ink cartridge
- patterned vellum
- glue stick or white craft glue
- soft eraser
- for variation: silver calligraphy marker, silver extra-fine-point marker, silver gel pen, plain vellum

ETIQUETTE ADVICE

At a formal event, cards directing guests to an assigned table or to individual seating assignments should have first and last names, as well as titles. In a more casual environment—a rehearsal dinner, an intimate or informal wedding, or the bride and groom's head table—first names only are acceptable.

1

• Sometimes a slight ink smudge can be removed by gently scraping the top layer of the paper with a craft knife. Don't write on the surface after removing the smudge. The ink will bleed.

• Attach vellum to the back of a light-colored card with a glue stick or white craft glue. They both dry clear. When working with a dark-colored card, apply the glue smoothly to the entire back of the card for an even finish.

STEP 1 Cut cards to size, or use packaged place cards from a stationer. Determine the position of the baseline, measure carefully, and draw a pencil line lightly onto the face of the card. If needed, draw guidelines to indicate the x-height, ascenders, and descenders. Using a broad-nibbed fountain pen, calligraph the guest's name onto the card.

STEP 2 Allow the ink to dry thoroughly. Gently remove any smudges. Carefully erase the pencilled guidelines.

STEP 3 Cut the vellum into pieces the exact size of the place cards. For the best fit, fold the cards and the vellum separately. Use a bone folder or the back of a spoon to get a good, crisp crease.

2

3

VARIATION True beginners can obtain dramatic results with metallic calligraphy markers and gel pens. The broad shape of the nib and heavier nature of a felt-tipped marker can't reproduce the delicate lines of pen and ink, but a light hand and a flair for embellishment produce a pleasing artistic effect, with or without a vellum overlay.

wedding
READING KEEPSAKE

Keep the memories of your wedding alive by transforming a passage from your ceremony into a work of art you can look at every day. You can choose a portion of your vows, a reading, or a meaningful wedding poem or song. A toast or blessing offered at the event would also work nicely. A touch of gold ink in the lettering adds distinction. Use a precut mat to frame the inscription. Painting flowers in a trail from the lettered sheet onto the mat ties the two together.

MATERIALS

• watercolor paper

• acid-free precut mat board

• pencil

• ruler

• broad-edged calligraphy pen

• fine-tipped calligraphy pen

• paintbrush

• black ink

• gold ink

• watercolor paint

• soft eraser

• masking tape

• light box (optional, see Tips and Techniques)

• for variation: braided satin upholstery rope, hot glue gun,

  fabric glue, purchased photo or memory album

1

TIPS AND TECHNIQUES

- If you do not have a light box, ink the letters directly over the initial pencil draft. Carefully erase the pencil lines once the ink has dried thoroughly.

- Press flowers from your wedding and attach them with diluted white glue or decoupage medium, instead of watercolor paint, to create the floral "bouquet."

- Any beautiful trim can be substituted to frame the text.

3

STEP 1 Cut the watercolor paper to fit the size of the mat opening, adding at least 1/2" (1 cm) on each edge for overlap. On a blank sheet of white paper, rule the working area that will show and add pencil rules to guide the size of the letters. Draft the words and flowers in pencil to work out the spacing.

STEP 2 Place the watercolor paper over the pencil draft on the light box. If needed, re-rule the pencil lines to guide the size of the letters. Using a fine-tipped pen, outline the first letter in black ink to create what is called an initial cap. Render the rest of the words in black ink, using a broad-edged pen.

STEP 3 Fill in the initial cap with gold ink. Add a dot of gold to the couple's names as a decorative element. Using a fine-tipped pen, add flourishes to the initial cap and first letters of the bride and groom's names, outlining the gold with a distinct shape. Paint the flowers on the watercolor paper.

VARIATION The same artwork creates a meaningful cover for a wedding photo album, memory book, or scrapbook. Attach the text sheet to the album using fabric glue or hot glue. Add a decorative border of upholstery trim using hot glue to give it a finished look.

CALLIGRAPHER HILARY WILLIAMS

f a v o r TAGS

Sending guests home with a token gift of appreciation has become a common practice at weddings. One way to personalize this gesture of gratitude is with calligraphic tags. Here, the gift tags are written in Uncial and are attached to small, geometric-shaped boxes. It is a good idea to place the favors on a table near the door for guests to take on their way out.

MATERIALS

- vellum
- white paper
- gift boxes
- 3/4" (2 cm) satin-edged ribbon—18" (46 cm) per favor
- pencil
- ruler
- broad-edged calligraphy pen
- black ink
- glue stick
- hot glue gun
- computer with scanner
- for variation: green, patterned vellum; gold paint marker; gold satin rope; hole punch

- Although Uncial is a heavy lettering style, when crafted with a thinner nib it looks delicate enough to pair with ornamental embellishments.

- A dab of hot glue on the ribbon's knot will keep it from opening accidentally.

- Try different pen nibs to test various weights for the final text.

STEP 1 Using the white paper, a pencil, and a ruler, draw the shape of the gift box and render the text.

STEP 2 Using a computer scanner, scan the renderings and delete the bottom tip of the cone. (A photocopier also works if you do not have access to a computer.) If you are trying more than one rendering or lettering weight, cut out both and place each on a favor box to see which looks better. Duplicate the tag of choice on the vellum, print the necessary quantity, and cut out the tags.

STEP 3 Fill a favor box and close it. Tie the ribbon into a bow at the top of the box. Use hot glue to adhere the wavy tails of the ribbon to the box. Attach the tag to the box using a glue stick. Be careful not to smudge the type.

VARIATION For variation, print the tags on colored, patterned vellum and cut out in a circle shape. Add a beautiful edge to the tag with a gold paint marker. Use a hole punch to create an opening. Pair with a different shaped box and gold satin rope instead of ribbon to completely change the appearance of this favor.

CALLIGRAPHER MELISSA DINWIDDIE
CRAFT ARTIST BETTE MATTHEWS

engagement
PARTY INVITATION

As soon as the engagement is announced, the parties for the couple begin. Choose an invitation style that is appropriate for the event, or even one that reflects the party location. Imitate the design of an illuminated manuscript and create a beautiful picture block paired with a classic, Blackletter text style. For this invitation, stationery was purchased with the graphic design preprinted on the paper and envelopes. After printing the invitation text, the sheet is trimmed to its final size.

MATERIALS

- grid paper
- white paper
- paper with preprinted graphic design
- matching envelope
- broad-edged calligraphy pen
- black ink
- spray mount
- computer with scanner
- for variation: clip art, white card, cream card

Anna I and Ramon

1

- Decorative papers can be purchased by the sheet at fine paper or stationery stores.

- Add a touch of gold to the design or to the lettering with gold calligraphy ink, a gold gel pen, or a gold paint pen.

- Rather than using a copy to paste up a centered mechanical, the rendered text can also be scanned into the computer and centered in a layout program.

Anni Marie La and Ramone Miguel

2

Anna Marie Lacroix
and
Ramone Miguel Perez
invite you to celebrate their engagement
Friday, the tenth of August
at seven o'clock in the evening

The Beaumont
One Chanterelle Circle

3

STEP 1 Working on grid paper at a comfortable working size, render each line of text for the final invitation. Align all rows at the left.

STEP 2 Make a good copy of the text on clean, white paper. Cut out each line. Using spray mount, center each line on a new sheet of grid paper to create a mechanical.

STEP 3 Scan the mechanical into the computer and reduce the text to the final size. Align the text so that it will fit on the paper in alignment with the preprinted artwork. Print the invitation.

VARIATION Instead of using paper with a preprinted design, create a picture block on plain paper with clip art. The look of the invitation will change dramatically based on the type of art selected and the color of paper and text.

CALLIGRAPHER MELISSA DINWIDDIE

wedding invitation
ETIQUETTE

In years past, the wedding invitation was a formal document that followed a strict formula in terms of its appearance and wording. Today, many couples still choose the classic invitation for their event. A variety of choices, however, are available—and appropriate—for a twenty-first century wedding. For most guests, the invitation is the first—and sometimes only—indication they'll receive about the style and formality of a wedding. Yours should reflect your personality as well as the wedding style, both in the presentation and the phrasing of the invitation.

Society's prescription for nuptial celebrations was clear-cut in previous decades. The bride's parents were the hosts, and the invitation came from them. A guest receiving a formal invitation for an event beginning after 6:00 P.M. understood that black tie was the appropriate attire, so it was unnecessary to include such a notation in the text. The invitation might request an R.s.v.p., and the guest would respond on his or her personal stationery. The invitation itself was for the wedding ceremony; if the guest was also invited to a reception, a separate reception card was included in the mailing.

Many of these customs are still utilized in the most formal of settings, but new standards of invitation etiquette have evolved to include a broader range of possibilities, reflective of the casual atmosphere of life today. Our modern social climate dictates that etiquette should be used as a guide only, rather than as a set of unbreakable rules. If your style is informal, or your wedding is informal, your invitation need not conform to any rules as long as all the necessary information is present and easy for the guest to understand.

SAMPLES OF INVITATION WORDING

THE BRIDE'S PARENTS HOST:
Mr. and Mrs. Matthew Beatty
request the honour of your presence
at the marriage of their daughter
Eliza Brook
to
Mr. Antoine Michel Richieu
Saturday, the fifth of June
at half after five o'clock
The Lynbrook Society for Ethical Culture
Lynbrook, New York

Reception following the ceremony

THE GROOM'S PARENTS HOST:
Mr. and Mrs. Jerard Richieu
request the honour of your presence
at the marriage of
Miss Eliza Brook Beatty
to their son
Antoine Michel Richieu
etc.

THE BRIDE'S PARENTS HOST AND
THE GROOM'S PARENTS ARE INCLUDED:
Mr. and Mrs. Matthew Beatty
request the honour of your presence
at the marriage of their daughter
Eliza Brook
to
Mr. Antoine Michel Richieu
son of Mr. and Mrs. Jerard Richieu
etc.

DIVORCED PARENTS HOST:
Mrs. Leanora Beatty
and
Mr. Matthew Beatty
request the honour of your presence
at the marriage of their daughter
Eliza Brook
to
Mr. Antoine Michel Richieu
etc.

DIVORCED AND REMARRIED PARENTS HOST:

Dr. and Mrs. John Hurst Lake

and

Mr. Matthew Beatty

request the honour of your presence

at the marriage of their daughter

Eliza Brook

to

Mr. Antoine Michel Richieu

etc.

BOTH SETS OF PARENTS HOST:

Mr. and Mrs. Matthew Beatty

and

Mr. and Mrs. Jerard Richieu

request the honour of your presence

at the marriage of their children

Eliza Brook

and

Antoine Michel

etc.

THE BRIDE AND GROOM HOST:

The honour of your presence is requested

at the marriage of

Eliza Brook Beatty

and

Antoine Michel Richieu

etc.

THE COUPLE HOSTS AND THE PARENTS ARE INCLUDED:

Together with their parents

Eliza Brook Beatty

and

Antoine Michel Richieu

request the honour of your presence

at their marriage

etc.

NONTRADITIONAL WORDING:

Eliza Brook Beatty

and

Antoine Michel Richieu

invite you to celebrate our wedding

or

invite you to gather in community

to witness and celebrate their marriage

or

invite you to share the joy

as we exchange marriage vows

or

invite you to dance at our wedding

etc.

or

Please join

Eliza Brook Beatty

and

Antoine Michel Richieu

at the celebration of their marriage

etc.

INVITATION ETIQUETTE TIPS

- As a standard rule of thumb, the people who pay for the wedding are mentioned on the invitation. Many couples, however, choose to honor parents by including their names, even if the parents are not making a financial contribution to the event.

- Write names out in full on an invitation or an envelope. Titles, such as Mister or Doctor, may be abbreviated.

- Traditionally, if the ceremony location is a house of worship, the phrase "request the honour of your presence" is used. When the ceremony takes place in a secular location, the phrase of choice is "request the pleasure of your company."

- The Anglican spelling of "honour" and "favour" is commonly used on wedding invitations, but "honor" or "favor" is perfectly acceptable.

- Spell out dates and times. Avoid using the abbreviations "P.M." or "A.M." For a starting time after 6:00 P.M., use the phrase "in the evening."

- Including the year after the date and the city after the location is optional.

- If your ceremony and reception are in the same location, a separate reception card is unnecessary. In the text, beneath the ceremony details, note "Reception immediately following."

- It is permissible to write R.s.v.p. in all capital letters, but this looks awkward in most scripts or calligraphic alphabets. Place this notation in the lower left corner of the invitation. If you are including a response card, do not include an R.s.v.p. notation in the invitation text.

- If a particular dress code is requested for the event, place the information in the lower right corner of the invitation. "Black tie," "Black tie encouraged," "Black tie optional," or "Casual attire welcomed" are all acceptable phrases.

- Send your invitations four to six weeks prior to the wedding. If you have international guests or many guests travelling a long distance, add two weeks. Guests are asked to respond one to two weeks prior to the event.

- Number your guest list. When sending out invitations, write in the guest's corresponding number on the back of each response card in pencil. That way, if someone forgets to write his name on the front of the response card, you can identify the guest by the number on your master list.

- To assemble, the enclosures are stacked face up on top of the invitation in the following order: the reception card, the response card (which should be slid under its envelope flap, not inserted into the envelope), and then any additional inserts, such as a pew card or driving directions. Insert the invitation and enclosures into the inner envelope (if using one), and insert the entire package into the outer envelope.

Elegant

Mr and Mrs Nicholas Carroll
145 Dearborn Street
Chicago, Illinois 60623

Mr and Mrs Nicholas Carr...
145 Dearborn Street
Chicago, Illinois 60623

Mr and Mrs Nicholas Carroll
145 Dearborn Street
Chicago, Illinois 60623

Table Five

Please join ...
at a rehearsal dinn...
in honor of

Lauren and Jim

Friday, the first of May
at five o'clock
Sundial Resort
Sanibel I...

4
Table

elegant CALLIGRAPHY

As a result of efforts to work more efficiently and to produce documents intended for daily use, alphabets branched out in many stylistic directions. Yet the general trend was towards a more flowing motion, culminating in the sinuous scripts of seventeenth-, eighteenth-, and nineteenth-century Europe. The advent of paper also allowed changes in options for both pen and ink, and new technologies spurred the development of the printed word.

Three alphabets are included in this chapter. When striving for elegance in your wedding, remember that an understated style sometimes has the biggest impact. Each of these refined alphabets is perfectly suited to an elegant style. French Gothic, created with the broad-edged pen, retains a sense of formality. Its thick and thin lines are formed by the angle of the pen and by the direction of the pen stroke. The other two—Bickham and Rook—are cousins, both created using the pointed pen. They originate from the copperplate-engraved texts used to teach basic writing skills. With a pointed pen, applied pressure, or lack thereof, is used to create the thick swells and delicate, thin lines common to this type of calligraphy.

In its heyday, the pointed pen was used for daily correspondence. It was commonly used with alphabets that reflected fine penmanship as much as fine calligraphy. Practice writing the letters with a pencil first, to get used to the shape of the letters and to be able to write them smoothly. The projects in this section show a variety of uses for the elegant lettering styles.

All scripts created with a fine-tipped calligraphy pen are similar in the way the letters are formed. Differences are subtle and may be noted in the flourishes of the capital letters, the ascenders, and the descenders. The thickness of lines is determined by the pressure applied to the strokes, not by the angle of the pen. This hand, based on a typeface known as Rook, uses round letters with loops in the capitals and long ascenders and descenders in the lowercase letters. It is a classic choice for an elegant wedding. CALLIGRAPHER NAN DELUCA

A B C D E F G H

I J K L M N O P Q

R S T U V W X Y Z

a b c d e f g h i j k l m

n o p q r s t u v w x y z

1 2 3 4 5 6 7 8 9 0

In the eighteenth century, master penman and engraver George Bickham published a book showing samples of his work and that of other masters from his time and previous centuries. It is still used today as a leading reference for script lettering and is an ideal choice for an elegant wedding. This alphabet honors him by bearing his name, Bickham. As with other script alphabets, it is created with a pointed pen, relying on pressure to produce the characteristic thick and thin lines. Its tailored capital letters rely on graceful swashes rather than looped flourishes; some of the lowercase letters have straight, rather than looped, descenders. CALLIGRAPHER SUSAN L. RAMSEY

A B C D E F G H
I J K L M N O P Q
R S T U V W X Y Z

a b c d e f g h i j k l m
n o p q r s t u v w x y z

1 2 3 4 5 6 7 8 9 0

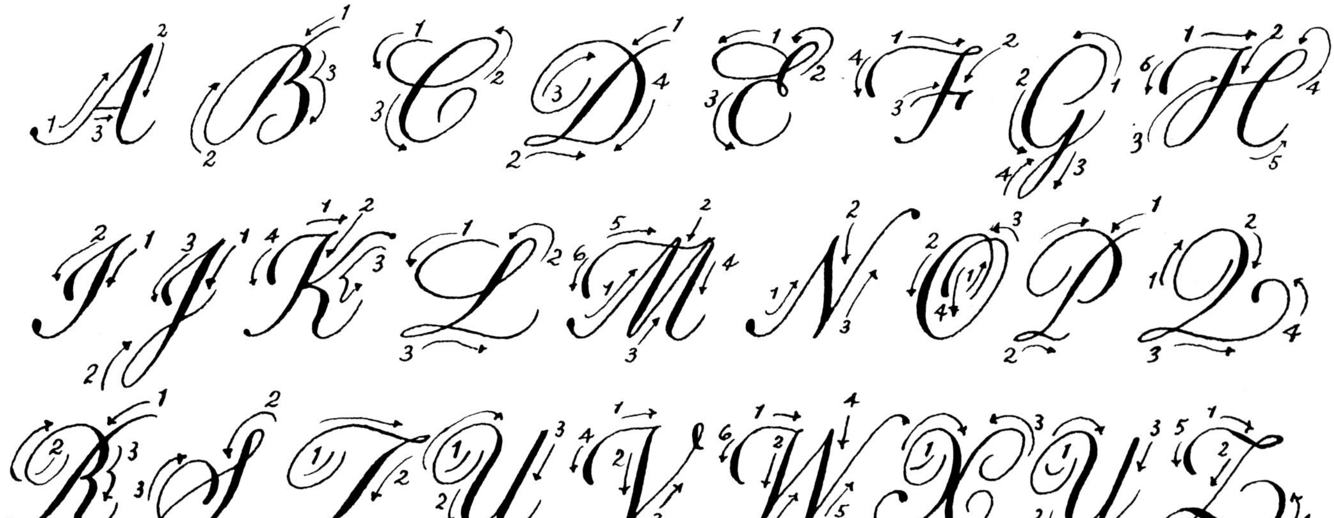

In the French Gothic, or Bâtarde, alphabet, the capitals are wide and round, with a fluidity of motion. Paired with closely packed lowercase letters, the effect is well-balanced. For this alphabet, use a broad-edged pen held at a 45-degree angle to the paper. A combination of this angle and the upright nature of the letters creates a heavy character that is sure to make your invitation and other wedding correspondence stand out.

CALLIGRAPHER SUSAN L. RAMSEY

ABCDEFGH
IJKLMNOPQ
RSTUVWXYZ

abcdefghijklm
nopqrstuvwxyz

1234567890

ABCDEFGH
IJKLMNOPQ
RSTUVWXYZ
abcdefghijklm
nopqrstuvwxyz
1234567890

r e h e a r s a l   d i n n e r
I N V I T A T I O N

There's no need to sacrifice elegance for a less formal event. A more relaxed event should still be announced with style. Here, a red, deckled edge emboldens a butter-colored card. For a small party, each card can be written by hand with beautiful script. Otherwise, scan an original hand-rendered invitation to duplicate. If you cannot find stationery with a border like the one shown here, you can apply a border to plain card stock and coordinating envelopes with calligraphy ink, paint, or even a metallic paint pen.

MATERIALS

for invitation with red, deckled edge:

- purchased card stock
- matching envelope
- fine-tipped pen
- black ink

for invitation with peach ribbon:

- petal paper
- vellum
- 1/8" (3 mm) wide peach satin ribbon
  —2 feet (61 cm) per invitation
- fine-tipped pen
- black ink
- hole punch
- computer with scanner

for invitation with white bow:

- patterned paper
- coordinating solid-colored paper
- vellum
- 3/8" (9 mm) wide white organza
  ribbon—1 foot (30 cm) per invitation
- fine-tipped pen
- black ink
- glue stick
- hole punch
- computer with scanner

for invitation with pressed flowers:

- watercolor paper
- pressed flower petals
- patterned art tissue paper
- white craft glue
- small, soft paintbrush
- fine-tipped pen
- black ink
- computer with scanner

for booklet variation:

- petal paper
- white paper
- 1/8" (3 mm) wide light green satin
  ribbon—18" (46 cm) per invitation
- fine-tipped pen
- black ink
- glue stick
- computer with scanner

VERSION 1 For this version, render the text, scan it into the computer, and print onto the vellum. Cut both the vellum and a sheet of petal paper to 4" x 8" (10 cm x 20 cm) in size. Place the printed vellum on top of the petal paper, and punch a series of small holes through both sheets at the top. Weave ribbon through the holes finishing with a bow on the left-hand side.

CALLIGRAPHER NAN DELUCA
CRAFT ARTIST BETTE MATTHEWS

TIPS AND TECHNIQUES

• Vellum may take longer to dry than paper and may smudge if handled at any point in time. Avoid touching the surface after it has been printed.

• Pressed flowers can be purchased at craft supply stores and some fine stationery stores. To make them, spread flower heads or petals on a paper towel so that they are not touching each other, and place another paper towel on top. Press between the pages of a phone book, adding weight to evenly press the pages. In two to three weeks, the flowers should be dry and pressed flat.

VERSION 2 Vellum softens the effect of the type here. Print the text onto patterned paper and mount it on a coordinating solid-colored paper using a glue stick. Allow for a 1/8" (3 mm) border. Cut a piece of vellum 1/4" (6 mm) shorter in length and width than the patterned paper and place it over the patterned paper. Punch two small holes at the top of the invitation, puncturing through all three sheets. Weave a white organza ribbon through the holes and finish with a petite bow.

VERSION 3 For this invitation, the text is printed onto watercolor paper that has been cut to size. Pressed flowers are adhered to the invitation with a diluted solution of white craft glue and water. Lightly brush glue solution on the backside of the flower. The invitation is wrapped in a patterned art tissue paper, allowing for a 1/2" (1 cm) overlap in front. Another pressed flower is glued to the front to keep the tissue closed.

VARIATION Create a booklet with the folded invitation inside. Use a glue stick to attach the invitation inside of the petal paper cover. Add a decorative ribbon along the spine.

e l e g a n t ENVELOPES

Calligraphy is frequently used to address an invitation envelope, whether the invitation itself has been penned by hand or produced by a printer. Although all styles of calligraphy look beautiful, penned script is probably requested most often for envelopes. Addresses may be placed centered, staggered, or flush left on the envelope.

MATERIALS

- envelopes
- guide sheet
- fine-tipped calligraphy pen
- black ink
- light box
- for variation: burgundy ink

ETIQUETTE ADVICE

Although some people choose to use a computer to address envelopes, simple, beautiful penmanship is preferable and far more personal. Other than titles, such as Mr., Mrs., and Dr., all names and words should be spelled out and not abbreviated. Although it is acceptable to abbreviate junior or senior (capitalizing the first letter of each), the most formal envelope would present the words spelled out in lowercase.

CALLIGRAPHER SUSAN L. RAMSEY

TIPS AND TECHNIQUES

• A heavy rule will show through a standard envelope, but a lined envelope will require working on a light box in order to see the inserted guide sheet. Alternatively, envelope lining can sometimes be removed—very carefully—and reinserted after the envelope has been addressed. This is extremely tedious and risks tearing the envelope or lining.

STEP 1 Draft a test envelope to work out the size and spacing of the letters and the lines. Once a pleasing arrangement has been determined, create a guide sheet of heavy lines, either with a marker or on a computer. Insert the guide sheet into the envelope. Determine the guideline that falls closest to the center of the envelope. This marks where the first line of the address should be placed. If an address contains a long line and you are using a staggered layout, the angle of the diagonal layout can be adjusted.

STEP 2 The zip code can be placed on the same line as the city and state, but sometimes it appears better when placed separately. Spreading out the spacing of the zip code looks very elegant.

STEP 3 Writing too close to any of the edges of the envelope is a common mistake. For an address with long lines, begin the first line more to the left, use a smaller angle for the diagonal layout, or drop the zip code down to a fourth line. Another common error is to place the address too high on the envelope. It will look better if the first line is centered both horizontally and vertically.

VARIATION You can use colored ink and understated flourishes to enrich the envelope without sacrificing the degree of formality.

reception
TABLE NUMBERS

The days of institutional numbers skewered onto stark, spiky metal holders to designate tables are over. The number on the table should be as beautiful as the place card itself, and calligraphy is a handsome way to achieve this effect.

The numbers can be displayed in many ways. Using folded cardstock, you can prop them as is. Small holders can be used for a more upright presentation. Or insert the inscribed paper into an elegant frame appropriate to the décor. Embellished with flourishes, the couple's new monogram, or a painted leaf or flower, these numbers do not have to be whisked away and hidden after the guests are seated.

MATERIALS

- paper or cardstock
- decorative frame
- table number holder or place card holder
- fine-tipped calligraphy pen
- fine brush
- black ink
- gold ink
- colored ink
- watercolor paint
- light box

ETIQUETTE ADVICE

Creating table assignments for guests is a thoughtful amenity. Although time-consuming (as well as thought provoking) for the wedding planner, it eliminates the need for guests to jockey for position upon arriving at the reception. It also rules out the possibility that Aunt Zelda may end up sitting by herself with your college sorority sisters because there was no room left at the family table.

VERSION 1 A number can stand alone nicely, but a bit of abstract watercolor flora makes a nice embellishment.

TIPS AND TECHNIQUES

• Because the table numbers must be readily visible, a fine-tipped calligraphy pen cannot create swells large enough to be proportionate to the necessary size of the numeral or lettering. There is a very simple solution to this. Render the text at normal size, enlarge it with a copier, and use a light box to trace the enlarged text onto the final card. Outline the letters or numbers and fill them in with ink with either a pen or a fine brush.

• Arrange tables in numerical order in the reception room so guests can find their spot with ease.

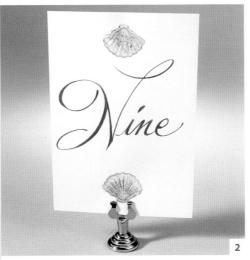

VERSION 2 Another option is to spell out the numeral and use color and art to tie into a theme. In this example, the card was designed for a sea-side wedding.

VERSION 3 Add the word "Table" to fill out the card. Flourishes and scrolls enhance the visual appeal.

VARIATION Glue the menu into a folded card and have the table number do double duty.

wedding
ANNOUNCEMENT

It's not uncommon to send an announcement after the wedding to acquaintances that were not invited to the event. The wedding announcement follows the basic format and wording of a wedding invitation and can vary in style in the same way. In the most formal style, the bride's parents announce their daughter's marriage to the groom, including the date and place of the wedding. This announcement was embellished with a graceful rubber stamp after it was printed on ecru card stock. A matching envelope is addressed using the same lettering style.

MATERIALS

• white paper

• ecru card stock

• pencil

• ruler

• broad-edged calligraphy pen

• black ink

• light box

• computer with scanner

• rubber stamp

• black stamp pad

• for variation: clear stamp pad, gold embossing powder

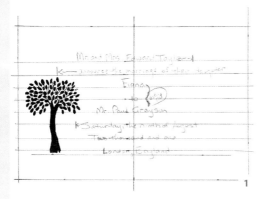

1

• Mistakes are easy to correct on projects that use the computer. Scan in corrections with patches of new text.

• The ink must be wet for embossing powder to stick to it, so work quickly. Do not overheat the powder: as soon as the gold begins to look glossy, remove it from the heat source.

Mr. and Mrs. Edw
announce the marriage of
Fiona

2

Mr. and Mrs. Edward Taylor
announce the marriage of their daughter
Fiona
to
Mr. Paul Grayson
Saturday, the ninth of August
Two thousand and one
London, England

3

STEP 1 Create a draft in pencil to work out the horizontal and vertical layout of the page. If adding any form of artwork to the final piece, include it in the draft to allow enough space for it.

STEP 2 Working on a light box, place a sheet of white paper over the pencil draft. Render the text.

STEP 3 When the text is finished, scan it into the computer. Print out the announcements on good card stock and trim to fit in the envelopes.

VARIATION Instead of stamping the design in black ink, use clear ink and immediately cover it with gold embossing powder. Tap off the excess and heat the embossed design until the powder is activated and begins to puff.

working with a
PROFESSIONAL
CALLIGRAPHER

Despite the best of intentions, sometimes the bride has little time to pursue a new course of learning, such as calligraphy, or to personally hand-letter envelopes, create last-minute place cards, etc. Instead, a bride may delegate the lettering of her wedding stationery to an experienced calligrapher. Choosing a professional to create all or part of the wedding stationery is a wise course of action in many instances. A professional understands the importance of the event and can handle it with expertise.

FINDING A CALLIGRAPHER

As with many wedding services, word of mouth is a great way to locate a trustworthy professional. Ask anyone you know who recently hosted or attended an event. Your reception hall, a local stationer, or wedding salon may also be of help. Look for ads or listings in regional wedding magazines. The Internet also offers a vast amount of information. For noteworthy web sites and other sources, including some of the book's contributors, refer to the Resources section on page 301. Don't feel as if you are confined to local sources only. With the ease of overnight delivery, fax, phone, and e-mail, any calligrapher is within your reach.

GUIDELINES

Have a clear idea of what you want before approaching the calligrapher. Artists often have portfolios of their work and can present you with new ideas, but it is important to know what you like first.

Be organized! The clearer your instructions, the more likely that the job will proceed without a hitch. Have every word on your address list correspond exactly with the way it is to be rendered. For example, write out "Mr. and Mrs." rather than using an ampersand. Write out "Street" and "Avenue" rather than abbreviating them, and spell out the names of states. Proofread your list before giving it to the calligrapher. Likewise, proofread their work before giving your final okay to the job.

COSTS AND CONTRACTS

Pricing varies greatly from region to region and artist to artist. Also, the cost of your work is dependent on what that work is. For example, hiring the calligrapher to create a master mechanical for your wedding invitation will have one cost. Contracting with the person to oversee the printing process will naturally be more expensive. Having the artist render each invitation individually will be even more costly. Choosing a design from the calligrapher's portfolio may be more cost-effective than asking for a completely new design. Hiring someone at the last minute will likely involve rush fees. Contracting with someone and canceling at a later date will sometimes result in a kill fee, or a loss of your deposit. Get a firm price quote in writing from the calligrapher and outline the entire job in a contract. This provides protection for both parties, clarifies the expectations, and helps avoid disappointment. Make sure the payment structure is clear and agreeable before signing a final contract. Some people require a deposit. Others may ask for a full payment prior to or upon delivering the finished work.

• Maintain realistic expectations. Many calligraphers are willing to match a typeface or imitate someone else's style, but calligraphy is similar to handwriting. Every person's penmanship is a little bit different.

• Look at the calligrapher's work and ask for samples, as quality and skill vary greatly.

• Book ahead! Calligraphers' schedules get busy, especially at certain times of year. Line up a calligrapher at least a month in advance of when you need the work done. Sooner is even better. Some calligraphers are booked several months in advance.

Romantic

...mance

...ic love happens; it is not
...ght about; one falls in love.

Robin and Erik
September 8, 2001

Heart

What comes from the heart
goes to the heart.

...bin and E...
...mber 8,...

Happiness

Happiness comes from
loving than being loved.

Robin and Erik
September 8, 2001

Promise

Love is a promise...
souvenir, once given...

...our friend...
...d are invited to...

...and...

...u we exchange...

Menu

Mixed Green Salad with Vegetables
&
Cold Poached Salmon with Dill Sauce
Orange Roughy with Beurre Blanc Sauce

romantic CALLIGRAPHY

CALLIGRAPHER HILARY WILLIAMS

The development of the printing press had profound impact on the penned word. Engravers, attempting to copy the work of calligraphers, developed a script style that, in turn, the calligraphers learned to copy with a fine-tipped pen. These scripts were sometimes embellished to the point of being illegible, and reflected the elaborate lifestyles favored by the upper classes in the seventeenth, eighteenth, and nineteenth centuries. The romance and grace of the earlier alphabets, however, was not lost. Artist William Morris brought the Italic hand back into the public eye in the late 1800s.

Calligraphy is romantic in and of itself, but the addition of embellishment, either in the letters or in the materials used, dresses up the printed word. The foundation for all pointed-pen script alphabets, Copperplate, is shown in this section, along with one of its offshoots. The letters for both scripts can be embellished with practice. The broad-edged, flourished Italic in this section is a romantic version of its simpler parent, adding a free-flowing swash to the Italic groundwork. Four projects in this section show beautiful applications for these romantic hands, from the simple menu, designed to make your guests' experience more pleasurable, to a collection of ideas for decorating place cards.

Italic refers to a slanted calligraphy form originally developed in the fourteenth and fifteenth centuries, that usually has connectives between the letters. The name Chancery Cursive is often used interchangeably, although it is a more ornate version of an Italic script. This flourished Italic is the calligrapher's own version of a Chancery Cursive and is sure to make an impression on your guests. The character of the flourishes and connectives adds deep drama to the letters without altering the basic structure or readability of the letters.

CALLIGRAPHER   BEVERLY WLADKOWSKI

ABCDEFGH
IJKLMNOPQ
RSTUVWXYZ
abcdefghijklm
nopqrstuvwxyz
1234567890

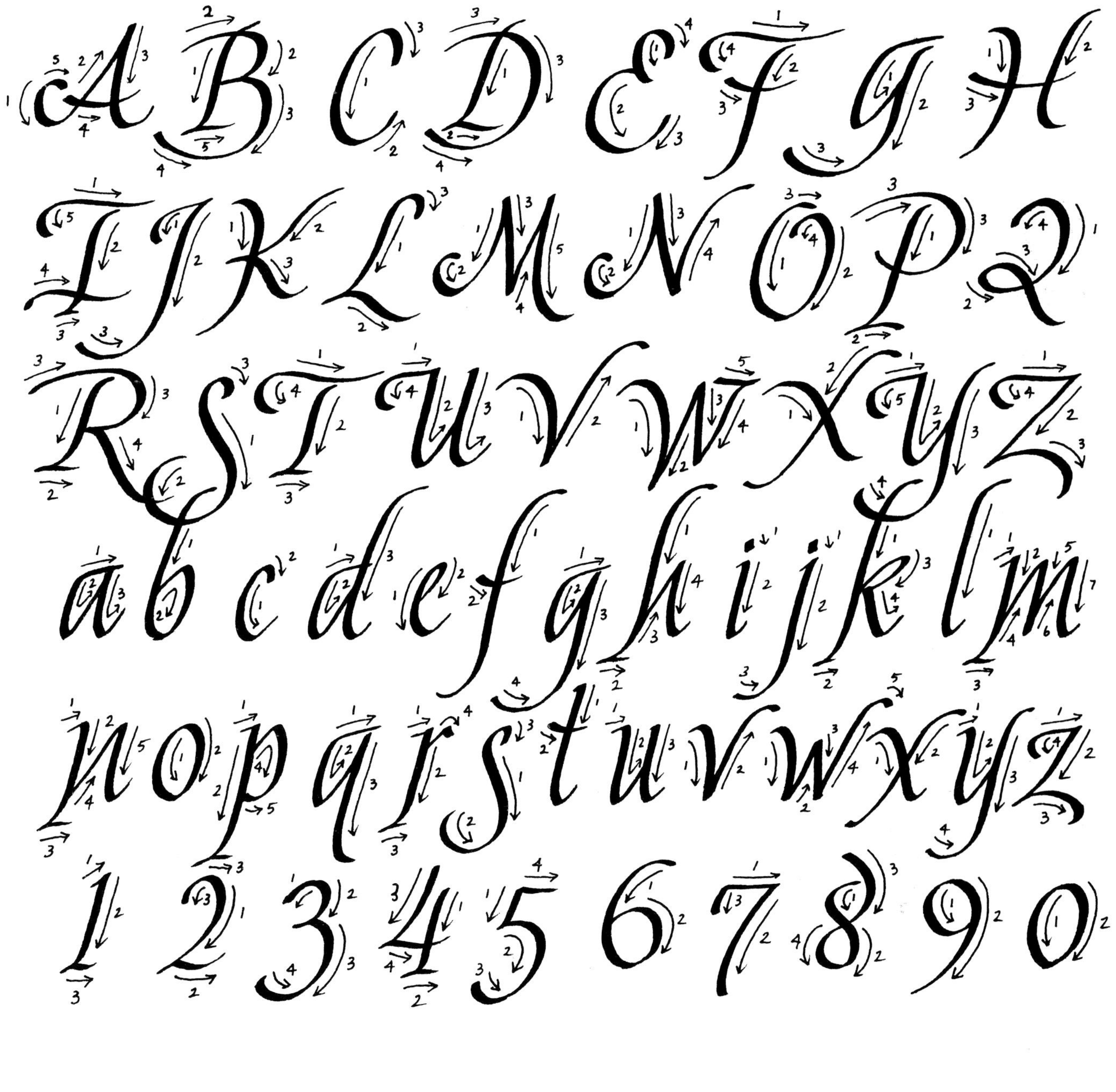

Copperplate script developed in conjunction with the invention of the printing press. Trying to duplicate the calligraphy of the penned word, engravers discovered quickly that they were better off designing a typeface specifically for their technology. The printing plates, engraved on sheets of copper with a pointed tool, created a new, even lettering form with delicate strokes, swells, and flourishes. Calligraphers gave up their broad-edged pen nibs and developed the pointed pen, with its fine-tipped nib, to copy the style of the copper plate engravings. In its simplest form or its most embellished—with ornate loops and swirls—Copperplate is a lovely choice for a romantic affair. CALLIGRAPHER HILARY WILLIAMS

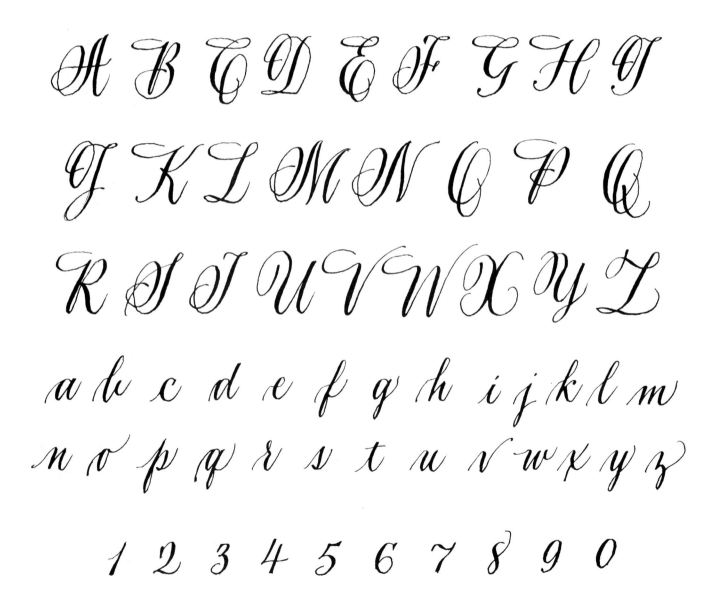

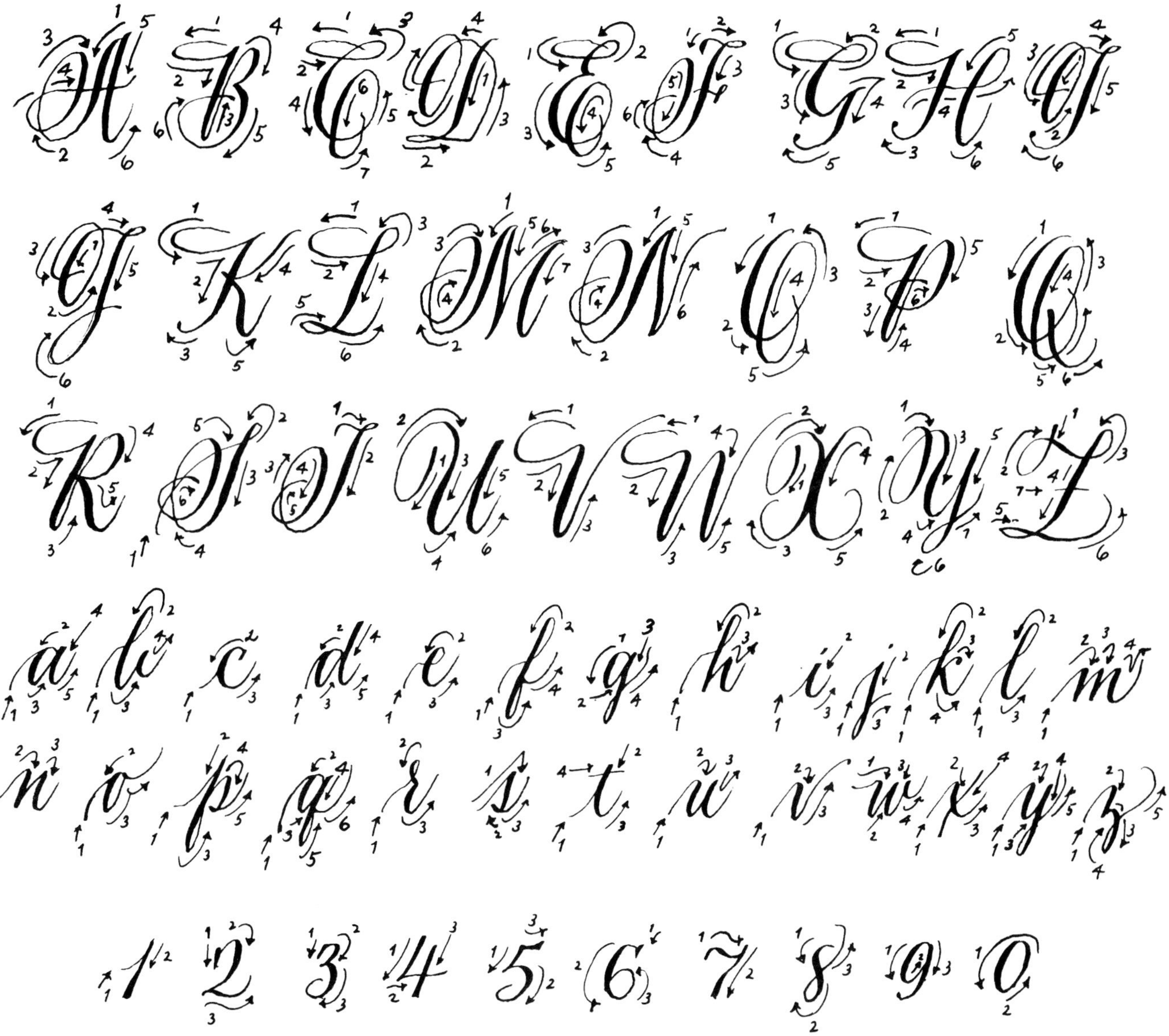

Another form of Copperplate, Spencerian is a rich, flowing script, perfectly symbolic of romance. For this particular alphabet, the pen rarely leaves the page and requires much practice to master the letters' graceful, fluid motion. As with other Copperplate scripts, the differences are seen mainly in the flourished capital letters as well as in the ascenders and descenders. CALLIGRAPHER HILARY WILLIAMS

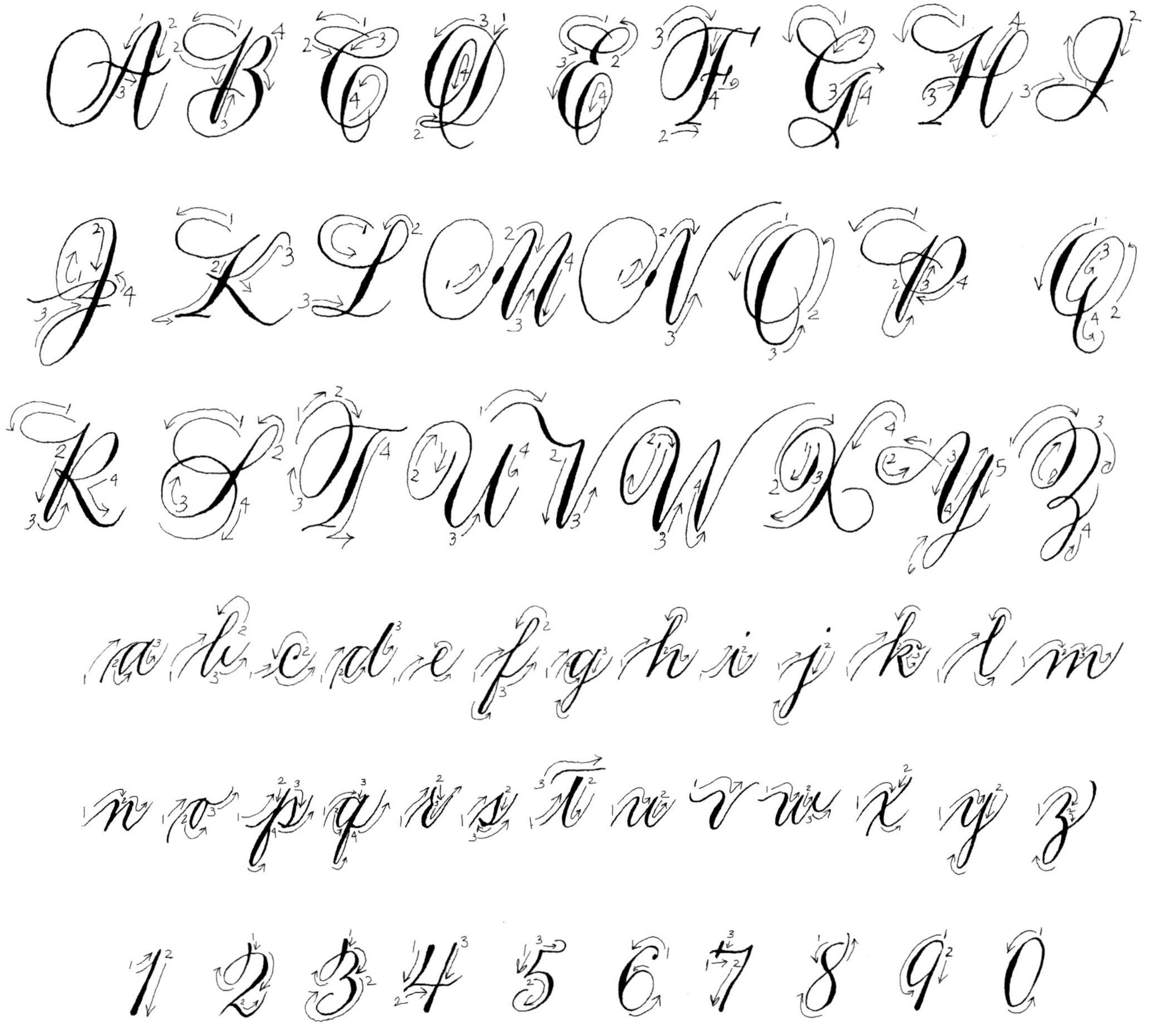
A B C D E F G H I
J K L M N O P Q
R S T U V W X Y Z
a b c d e f g h i j k l m
n o p q r s t u v w x y z
1 2 3 4 5 6 7 8 9 0

scroll INVITATION

An unusual and unique way to present a wedding invitation, the scroll automatically conjures up images of medieval proclamations and Renaissance feasts, town criers, nobility at court, and all of Shakespeare's romantic characters. The soft, mottled surface of today's parchment is perfectly suited for this project. Despite its slight translucence, it is very strong. Using a flourished, Italic hand for the text adds to the historic aura and romance of the document. A contrasting paper or paper-backed fabric set behind the parchment creates contrast for the mailed invitation, which is rolled into a scroll, tied with ribbon, and inserted into a mailing tube. It is difficult to write directly onto a cylinder, so use good-quality mailing labels to address each tube.

MATERIALS

- parchment paper
- paper-backed brocade fabric
- organza ribbon—12" (30 cm per invitation)
- mailing tube
- labels
- broad-edged calligraphy pens
- black ink
- pencil
- soft eraser
- computer
- light box
- for variation: gold ink

Because you have shared in our lives
by your friendship and love
you are invited to share with us...

Sarah Lynn Chambers

and

Michael James Foss

When we exchange marriage vows
and begin our new life together
on Saturday, the ninth of June
two thousand and one
at half past two o'clock in the afternoon
Clairmont Country Club
Clairmont, Maryland

Reception immediately following ceremony

1

TIPS AND TECHNIQUES

• If you do not have a computer, draft the text with pencil on paper that is the same size as the finished invitation. Write over the pencil draft quickly with pen to help decide spacing. Cut the draft into separate lines; then paste or tape the lines onto another sheet of the same size to center the text. Use this as the master draft.

• Although a light box makes this project easier, it is not completely necessary. Set the text of the computerized document in a very heavy type if a light box is not available. Parchment paper is somewhat translucent, so the bold image from the computer printout should show through.

• Check with your local Post Office to see if there are any special requirements for mailing tubes, such as the required size and method of wrapping or sealing the tube.

• The brocade fabric shown here is backed with paper and was purchased as an 8 1/2" x 11" (22 cm x 28 cm) sheet in a specialty paper store.

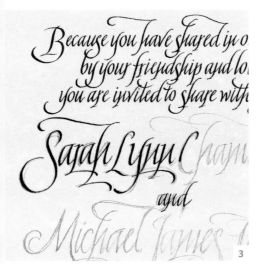

2

3

STEP 1 Using a computer, type the invitation text into a document. Set margins to make it the same size as the finished invitation. Center the text and add line breaks. Use fonts similar in size and spacing to the calligraphic alphabet for the finished product. This layout may require several drafts to get it right.

STEP 2 Place the computer printout on your light box and a piece of parchment paper on top of it, so the printout can be seen through the parchment. Follow the size and placement of the computer type as a guide for lettering the invitation onto the parchment. Lightly pencil-in the names of the bride and groom matching the shapes of the calligraphic letters.

STEP 3 Begin to write the text portion of the invitation in ink. Omit the names of the bride and groom but ink the "and" between them. When the text is dry, use a larger nib on the calligraphy pen to add the couple's names. Allow to dry thoroughly. Carefully erase the pencil guides.

VARIATION For an extra decorative touch, write the names of the bride and groom in gold ink.

guest table NAMES

One of today's popular wedding trends is to assign a name, rather than a number, to each reception table as a means of informing guests of their seating assignments. Tables can be named after cities where the couple has vacationed, hobbies or interests, romantic song titles, or, as presented here, words relating to love and marriage. In addition to the table name, include a few thoughts, a poem, or a quotation related to the word's theme. Place the table name in a beautiful frame worthy of display throughout the reception.

MATERIALS

• picture frames with freestanding easel back

• watercolor paper

• watercolor paint

• pencil

• fine-tipped calligraphy pen

• black ink

• soft eraser

ETIQUETTE ADVICE

It may be more difficult for guests to find their seats when tables are identified with names instead of numbers, especially at a large wedding with many tables. Consider providing a calligraphic map next to the escort cards, showing the location of each table name in the room. Alternatively, ask an usher, bridesmaid, or member of the catering staff to stand near the entrance and direct guests to the correct area in the room.

1

TIPS AND TECHNIQUES

• Flowers can be painted to sit behind the text or to frame it around the borders. If planning to render text over a painting, be sure that the text is legible.

• Watercolor paper has a soft, giving finish that erases cleanly. Be gentle when erasing so as not to damage the paper's surface or smudge the illustration or lettering.

STEP 1 Measure and cut the watercolor paper to fit the frame. Paint a flower in the center of the card using watercolor paint or calligraphy ink.

STEP 2 When the watercolor paint is completely dry, add rules as guides for sizing the letters. Draft text in pencil to work out the spacing.

STEP 3 Render the text using a fine-tipped calligraphy pen and black ink. Let the ink dry thoroughly before erasing pencil marks.

2

3

VARIATION In addition to changing the name of each table, paint a different flower on each card to add visual interest. Any favorite flowers can be applied, or choose flowers that coordinate with those used in the centerpieces.

combination
PLACE CARDS

Place cards, also known as escort cards, are used to indicate a guest's seating assignment. They are often the first detail encountered when entering a wedding reception. Beautiful calligraphy adds a touch of romance to any card. The combination of writing the first name in a fine-tipped Copperplate script at a jaunty angle and writing the last name with a block print using a broad-edged Italic nib gives the card further interest. Cards can be purchased in various colors and sizes.

MATERIALS

for unadorned place cards:

• **purchased place cards**

• **black ink**

• **fine-tipped calligraphy pen**

• **broad-edged calligraphy pen**

for burgundy place cards:

• **purchased place cards**

• **gold paper**

• **gold ink**

• **fine-tipped calligraphy pen**

• **broad-edged calligraphy pen**

• **decorative hole punch**

• **glue stick**

for flower-studded place card:

• **purchased place cards**

• **black or colored ink**

• **silk flower bud (or watercolor paint and fine paintbrush)**

• **fine-tipped calligraphy pen**

• **broad-edged calligraphy pen**

• **glue gun**

for ribboned place card:

• **purchased place cards**

• **blue ink**

• **6" (15 cm) of ribbon per card**

• **fine-tipped calligraphy pen**

• **broad-edged calligraphy pen**

for variaton:

• **purchased place cards**

• **black ink**

• **fine-tipped calligraphy pen**

• **broad-edged calligraphy pen**

VERSION 1 Gold ink adds dramatic interest to a burgundy place card. Use a decorative hole punch to tie the cards to a theme or season. Back the decoratively punched card with a small piece of paper in a contrasting color or one that coordinates with the ink color. Adhere with a glue stick. Alternatively, attach the cutouts to the card, allowing them to extend over the top of the fold.

• Tent cards are available prepackaged in office supply and stationery stores or can be ordered to match other wedding stationery items. Any fine quality, heavyweight paper that will hold ink well can be cut to size and folded to make handmade cards.

• Ribbons come in every size, color, and fabric you can imagine. Organza, tulle, silk, and satin are particularly romantic. French wired ribbons will hold any shape they are placed in, while ribbons without wires have a natural bounce when tied into a bow.

VERSION 2 A delicate flower painted onto a place card adds grace and beauty. As an alternative, attach a three-dimensional bud using a silk or dried flower. Adhere with hot glue.

VERSION 3 Anchor a beautiful bow by punching two holes close together in the upper left corner of the card. Choose a wide ribbon for a lavish effect or a narrower ribbon for a more tailored look. The long tails of the ribbon create a veil over the guest's name. Colors can coordinate or contrast.

VARIATION Practice makes perfect, and a practiced hand can embellish a card with pen alone. Elaborate flourishes complement the script lettering and need no additional decoration.

CALLIGRAPHER HILARY WILLIAMS
VARIATION CALLIGRAPHER SUSAN L. RAMSEY
CRAFT ARTIST BETTE MATTHEWS

menu CARD

Whether the meal is a luncheon buffet or a sit-down dinner, telling the guests what is being served is always appreciated. Menu cards can be displayed on the table the same way that table numbers are, or a menu can be placed at each table setting. Lettered with beautiful script, the cards are beautiful on their own. To embellish them even more, add a painted flower, or wrap the card in a beautiful tissue and finish with a bow.

MATERIALS

- white paper
- card stock
- art tissue
- ribbon for bow
- watercolor paint
- black ink
- fine paintbrush
- fine-tipped calligraphy pen
- tape
- light box
- computer with scanner
- for variation: petal paper

Mixed Green Salad with Vegetables
Cold Poached Salmon with Dill Sauce
Orange Roughy with Buerre Blanc Sauce
Sliced Roast Beef with Rosemary au Jus and Horseradish Sauce
Oven Roasted Turkey Breast with Cranberry Chutney
Chicken Cacciatore

1

TIPS AND TECHNIQUES

• Long lines of text can be difficult to render in a straight line. Adding rules to indicate the baseline and waistline will help guide your hand as well as keep track of the x-height for the letters.

• Adding dingbats, or small, decorative ornaments, between the menu sections helps to visually break up text and organize the menu elements into courses or food groups.

Mixed Green Salad with Vegetables

Cold Poached Salmon with Dill Sauce
Orange Roughy with Buerre Blanc Sauce
Sliced Roast Beef with Rosemary au Jus and Horseradish Sauce

2

Mixed Green Salad with Vegetables

Cold Poached Salmon with Dill Sauce
Orange Roughy with Buerre Blanc Sauce
Sliced Roast Beef with Rosemary au Jus and Horseradish Sauce
Oven Roasted Turkey Breast with Cranberry Chutney
Chicken Cacciatore
Sauteed Chicken Marsala

Choice of Penne, Rigatoni or Farfalle Pasta
with Vodka, Marinara or Bolognase Sauce

Double Baked Potatoes
Wild Rice
Haricots Verts Bundles
Assorted Crusty Breads and Rolls

Viennese Dessert Table
Ice Cream Sundae Bar
Wedding Cake
Coffee and Tea Service

3

STEP 1 Create a draft for the text on a computer using a typeface similar in size and spacing to the lettering style you have chosen. Add rules to use as guidelines for each line.

STEP 2 Placing the draft on a light box and the white paper on top, render the text. Adjust the horizontal and vertical layout by cutting the text and taping it to the card stock in proper alignment to create a mechanical.

STEP 3 Scan the mechanical, clean up the edges and tape marks, and print the menu on card stock.

VARIATION An interesting method of displaying the menu is to roll it around each guest's napkin like a napkin ring. Use petal paper or vellum to match the colors used throughout the room.

SUSAN L. RAMSEY
CHRISTOPHER J. WATKINS
HILARY WILLIAMS

a fine ROMANCE

A wedding oozes romance. This is not the time to be shy about showing emotion. What does "romance" mean to you? Is it soft, sentimental, nostalgic, sweet? How would that feeling translate into something more tangible? Here are a few ideas to consider.

For starters, choose a lettering style that fits the bill. The more ornate, the more romantic it is. The passionately flourished capitals, ascenders, and descenders of pointed-pen scripts connect and intertwine, mimicking the joining of two lives and families. But don't ignore the broad-edged pen alphabets. The sweeping swashes of a flourished Italic are as romantic as any Copperplate and bring to mind the grace of Renaissance times.

Incorporate passages of romantic poetry into the invitation or menu. Add love quotes to place cards. Name the tables after famous couples. Inscribe romantic passages in beautiful calligraphy on place mats, table runners, or napkin rings made of exquisite paper.

Sophistication and elegance are always romantic, yet tasteful adornment can add to the effect. Ribbon is a simple complement that packs a romantic wallop. Tie together more than one for a multicolored bow, or tie the ends into a cluster of love knots. Weave ribbons into a patchwork for your program cover or to decorate the place card table. Wrap your invitation in lace or brocade, or create ruffles of organza, tulle, satin, or luscious silk to adorn almost anything. A table full of favors wrapped in sumptuous fabrics with tags of sweeping calligraphy creates a romantic display.

Flowers are romantic in any form and can be incorporated in many ways. Add a delicate, fresh blossom to place cards, a handful of dried lavender to invitation envelopes, or a garland painted with watercolor to adorn your envelopes.

Use color judiciously for a whisper of romance. A touch of gold, opulent and regal, enriches lettering or materials. Pastel colors murmur and blush, adding a suggestion of endearment.

Finally, find a way to make it personal. Incorporate family traditions into the wedding details. Display wedding photos of family members with a sign rendered in beautiful script explaining who's who. Create a calligraphic family tree or timeline of the couple's lives. Giving guests even a hint of the intimate affection shared by bride and groom will pull on each and every heartstring.

By all means, use discretion. Don't overdo any of these ideas, as too much of a good thing will definitely push your work beyond the limits of good taste.

• Seal the envelopes with sealing wax.

• Add a hint of perfume to the invitation.

• Buy the beautiful "Love" postage stamps for mailing invitations.

• Place the guest book on a bed of rose petals.

Modern

Please join us for a
Post Wedding Brunch
sunday, November twenty-third at twelve noon
at the home of
Ethan and Alexandra Foe
103 Fifth Avenue
Apartment 801

Regrets only
12-333 7463

& Sparks invite you to witness
the marriage of their daughter

Peter Lincoln Holbrook

the sixth of September
afternoon

modern CALLIGRAPHY

CALLIGRAPHER MELISSA DINWIDDIE

In the twentieth century, mass-produced, printed matter became cost efficient. Consequently, new typefaces were being developed constantly. With the advent of the personal computer, handwriting practically became obsolete. Classic, elegant, romantic, and artistic—these words easily can be used to categorize the calligraphic form. Applying the word "modern" almost seems like an anomaly. Yet, in the grand scheme of calligraphy's history, alphabets developed to copy twentieth-century typefaces can certainly be considered modern.

The art of letters has come full circle. Each generation looks to the past, selectively choosing styles that are appealing and adapting them to modern sensibilities. Traditional form becomes updated. In today's world, there is a whole new breed of weddings, and you can successfully pair a calligraphic style with your forward-thinking attitude. The modern Italic shown here is an updated version of the classic, while the French Rondo is based on a typeface in wide use today. Clean lines, interesting materials, bold colors, and progressive design all contribute to overall appearance, updating calligraphy for the twenty-first century wedding.

Searching for a lettering style for one of her own invitations, this calligrapher used an invitation she found in a magazine as a jumping-off point and developed this unique, modern, Italic hand. Although it has a distinct "brush" quality, it is created with a broad-edged pen and many pen twists, particularly on the exit strokes of the letters. To attain the finest hairlines, she drags a bit of wet ink with one corner of her pen nib.

CALLIGRAPHER MELISSA DINWIDDIE

A B C D E F G H
I J K L M N O P Q
R S T U V W X Y Z
a b c d e f g h i j k l m
n o p q r s t u v w x y z
1 2 3 4 5 6 7 8 9 0

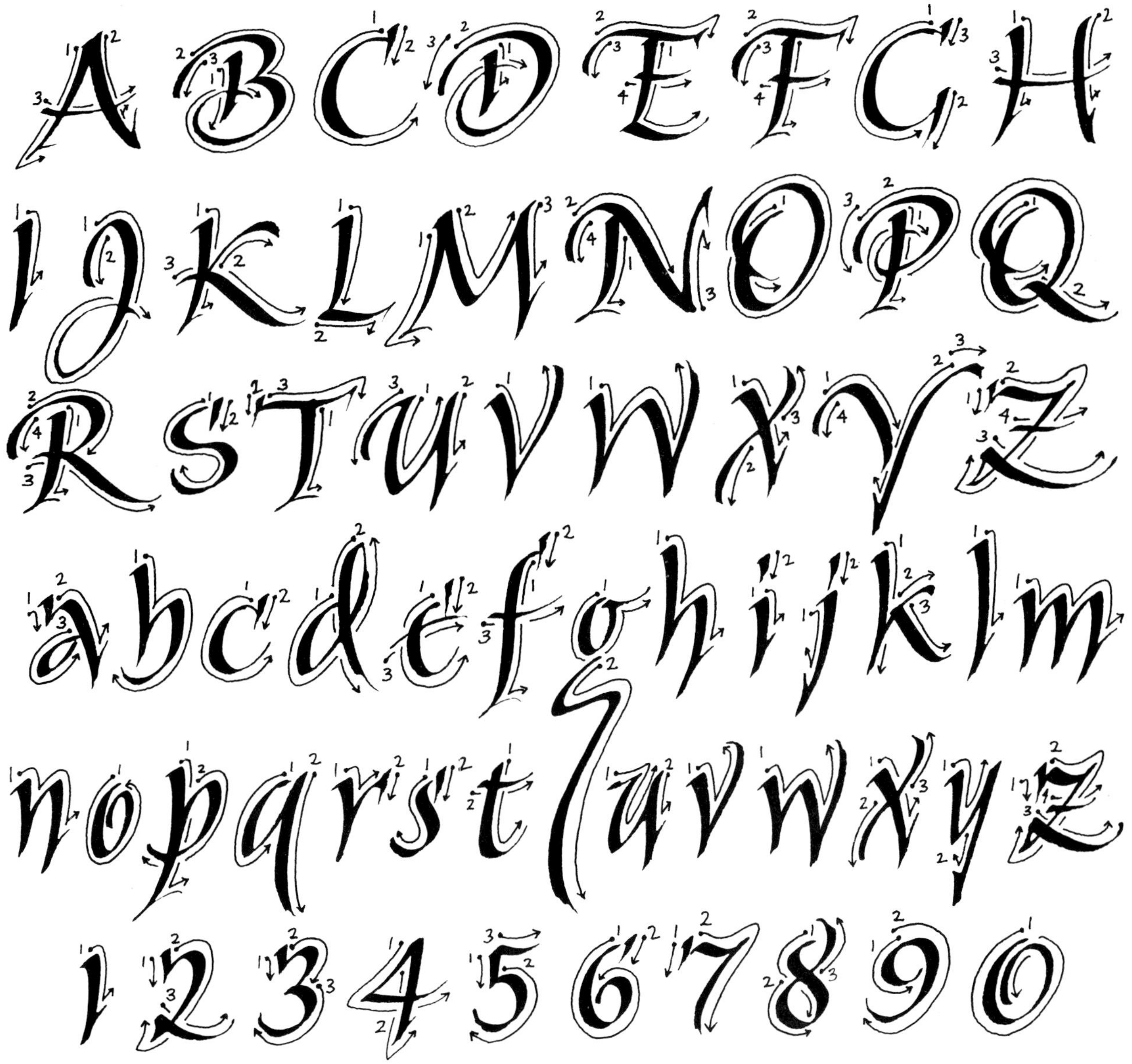

Sweet and charming without being overly fussy or outdated, this nostalgic style shows us that everything old can be new again. Its clean lines are similar to some of today's most popular typefaces. Created with a broad-edged pen, the round, vertical letters of this uncluttered alphabet gives a modern interpretation of the seventeenth-century Ronde style. CALLIGRAPHER LISA J. KENNEDY

A B C D E F G H
I J K L M N O P Q
R S T U V W X Y Z

a b c d e f g h i j k l m
n o p q r s t u v w x y z

1 2 3 4 5 6 7 8 9 0

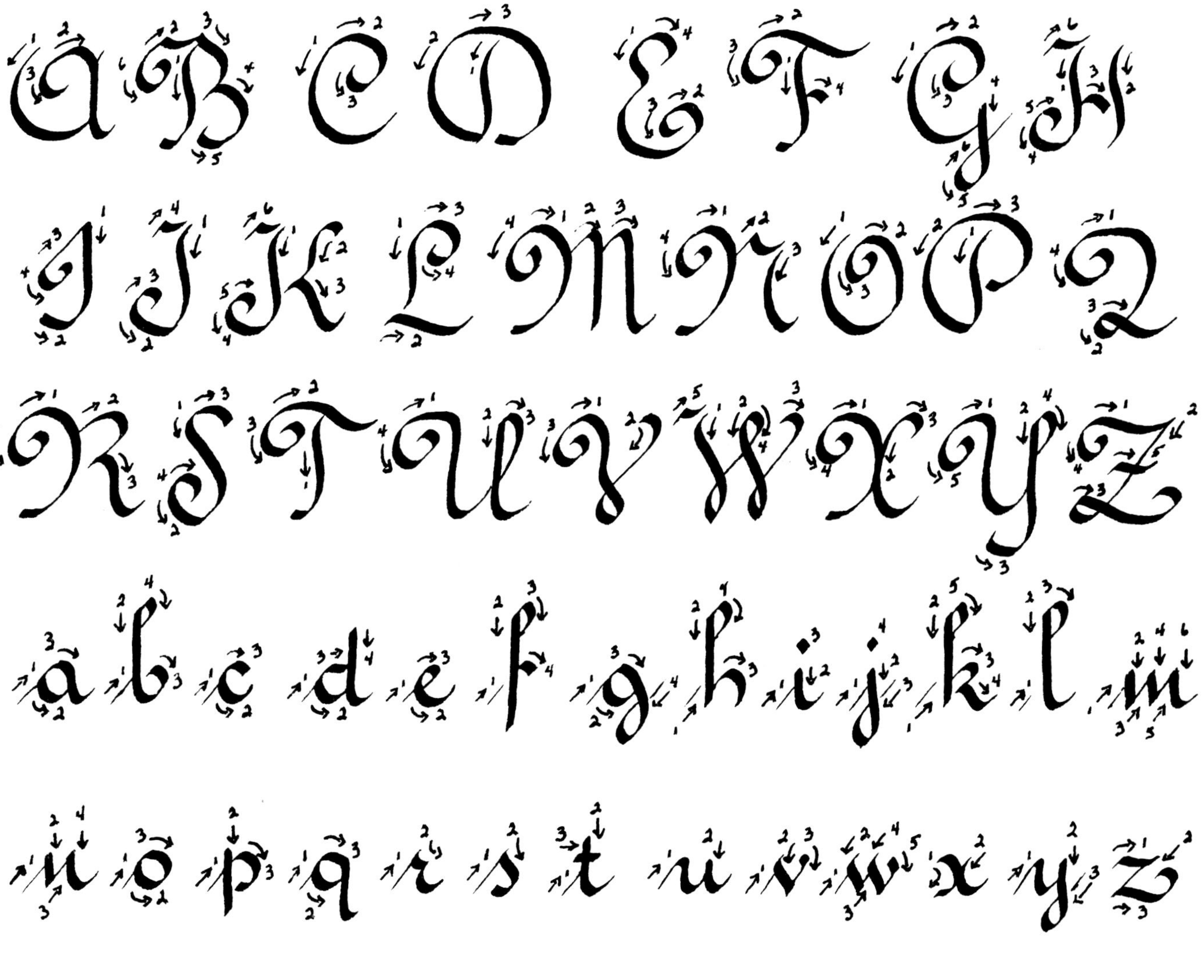

initial TAGS

Favors are a charming way to thank guests for attending the wedding. Bags made of hand-made paper and silver skeleton leaves are a fun and simple way to package your favors. Decorating with handmade tags adds a nice personal touch. The tags here show the bride's and groom's first initials rendered in the modern Italic alphabet along with the wedding date. The couple's new monogram would be a lovely alternative. The tag is attached with a coordinating silver organza ribbon threaded through two holes in the top of the bag and tied into a lively bow. Place them directly on the tables at each place setting.

MATERIALS

- white paper
- watercolor paper
- purchased favor bags
- 2" (5 cm) wide organza ribbon—18" (46 cm) long per bag
- broad-edged calligraphy pen
- black ink
- computer with scanner
- scissors
- hole punch
- for variation: pinking shears or decorative-edge scissors

ETIQUETTE ADVICE

Favors can be placed at each setting on the table, handed to guests at any point during the reception, or left at the door for them to take on their way out. Although it may seem obvious that the gift is meant for the guest, when leaving favors unattended, provide a sign or incorporate the information into the tag to eliminate any ambiguity.

1

• Use a photocopier instead of a scanner to enlarge or reduce the size of the mechanical and duplicate the tags en masse.

2

3

STEP 1 Render the text to create a mechanical, using a broad-edged calligraphy pen and black ink.

STEP 2 Scan the text into a computer layout program and try it in different configurations, altering the size and placement of the text as well as the shape of the tag. Cut the tags out and test them with the favor bag to find the most pleasing arrangement.

STEP 3 Duplicate the chosen tag in the document. Then print out as many as needed on watercolor paper. Cut them out, and punch a hole at one end for the ribbon.

VARIATION Choose a petal paper bag and a colored ribbon to incorporate wedding colors into the favors. Experiment with pinking shears or decorative-edged scissors when cutting out the tags.

CALLIGRAPHER MELISSA DINWIDDIE
CRAFT ARTIST BETTE MATTHEWS

Wedding Favors and Decorations

A celebration sounds like fun. Whether it's dancing far into the night (or morning), a feast for the masses, or candlelight and sophisticated ambiance, you want everyone to be filled with joy and to share in the excitement. Too often, a celebration can become overwhelming if you're the one throwing it and organizing all the details. Let's face it, it can take a lot of work to give the impression of fun. A little stress is livable—we know you deal with a modicum of pressure with your usual panache every day of your stylish life. Navigating normal tensions is par for the course of modern lives. However, head too far down the path of managing minutia, and the enjoyment begins to fizzle. Why give equal weight to every single element of a wedding, anyway? Details are only charming and enjoyable when they don't take over your life, so keep a level head and don't try to do it all. It is possible to keep it fun. After all, there is little sense in spending as much energy on napkin rings as you do on the guest list. Reigning in obsessive tendencies will go a long way to ensure a positive experience as you prepare for the wedding. Details and crafts are a great way to leave your mark—let it be a vivacious, happy, and calm one. It's all about creating an experience and having fun—through the planning *and* partying process.

It comes as no surprise, we're sure, that weddings are a prime example of complicated enjoyment—it looks like sweetness and light, but it can take hours of reworking (and overworking) the details to get everything right. The appearance of happenstance or coincidental details—that everything is falling together "just so" as if it were a happy accident—takes loads of attention, control, and practice. You have to be wise and figure out what is really worth it. Make elements for your wedding that mean something to you—but don't over-commit to a craft.

Why do some brides get a reputation for lacking humor as they plan their weddings? We can't be sure, but we have a suspicion is has something to do with hand-embossing every piece of paper with the image of a flower. What happens when you do that? You're forced to carry the embossing through to everything, lest it all look unfinished; you give up your time and conversation to make sure it gets done; and, what started as a nice gesture of spring has become a demanding floral beast. We want you to let yourself off the hook. Crafts are not supposed to make you edgy or rubber stamp–crazed. Quite the opposite. Making items for your wedding celebration can give you some automatic quiet time—some chance to sit, focused on one task instead of juggling a million things. It lets you connect with your spouse-to-be and your guests, too. Planning ahead and sticking to your ideas will help prevent you from overdoing it.

Making something by hand is a thoughtful gesture. But that doesn't mean you have to do everything yourself. There is a reason why there are so many wedding industry professionals around—because it is difficult for one person to do it all. For all the elements you make by hand, you are probably saving money—but you are spending something else just as valuable: your time and energy. You need to decide from the get-go how much money, time, and energy you have in your budget. Be realistic about how much of these three resources will be spent on each element. Spend too much of any of them and your enjoyment suffers, and so does that of many of your closest cohorts. It's all about balance.

Remember that while planning a wedding, there will be dinners, cocktails, picnics, and parties that crop up. Don't overschedule yourself and miss out on the good things in life. Take on what is special to you and leave the rest to professionals, wedding planners, a group of talented friends, and mail order. Try to limit the handmade items to things that cannot be purchased, or that you would have to go without for budgetary reasons.

It will be a breeze to incorporate your inimitable style into your wedding.

The guests already know and like you. They know your kooky taste in color combinations, your penchant for salsa music, and the ever present yellow flowers at your house. Don't let them down. A formal occasion does not mean you rewrite your personality—it means you amplify it and suit the event to fit.

We've given you options here for unique celebration ideas. Dress up a table, direct people to their seats, decorate the area, and amuse people. A good way to tackle it? Read the directions and go. A better way? Look through the projects and adapt them to fit you. We've avoided showing examples in the lacy white floral style—not because it is ill suited for these projects, but because you've probably seen enough of that to adequately adapt to that look if it's your bag. If it's not, we've given you a head start on a pleasant, modern deviation.

Lucky in Love Treats
PEARLY CHOCOLATE FAVORS

Sweetness is a theme for the day. A wedding can be a casual affair, a formal mass, or a party until dawn. All forms, though, obviously contain expressions of love. Echo that sweet sentiment without getting syrupy. Chocolates are sophisticated, and they are familiar elements in courtship (chocolates on Valentine's Day, bon-bons after a date), but they are still plenty of fun for both young children and adults. Make a twist on a traditional gift by dusting the molded chocolates with luster powder, a food-safe confectioner's supply that is made to give sweets a jewel-like finish.

DIRECTIONS

1. Prepare packaging first by cutting a piece of corrugated paper board to fit your candy bags. Press foil over board and trim excess. Slip board into candy bag and set aside.

2. Melt chocolate tablets in double boiler or microwave (follow directions on package).

3. Spoon chocolate into candy mold.

4. Tap mold to even out the chocolate and get rid of air bubbles.

5. Let cool until set. (You can put it in the refrigerator for 10 to 15 minutes if you're in a hurry.)

6. Pop chocolates out of molds and arrange faceup on a clean surface. Wear gloves to protect the candies from fingerprints and melting.

> **TIP** *Too much hassle to melt and mold chocolate? (It's really very easy, though.) Buy your favorite chocolates and dress them up.*

MATERIALS

chocolate buttons or tablets (available at cooking stores or candymaking section of craft supply stores)

cranberry luster dust, green pearl dust (white dust with a slight greenish hue) (see p. 76 for references.)

candy mold

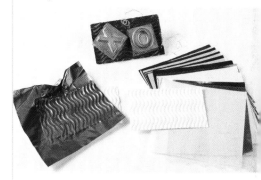

corrugated paper

plastic coated silver wire

foil candy wrappers

plastic treat bags

scissors or craft knife

new paintbrush (dedicated to candy decorating)

double boiler or microwave

thin vinyl or latex kitchen gloves

7. Brush luster dust on chocolates.

8. Put chocolates in wrappers and fold top edge to back; close with twists of wire, or seal with a sticker.

TIP *Use a mix of dark chocolate and milk chocolate. The soft, round flavor of the milk chocolate will make it palatable for most people, but the toasty, forceful flavor of the dark chocolate adds a depth that assures the favor won't be a cutesy candy but, rather, an elegant treat.*

VARIATION

Particularly fun for kids are chocolate pops. What is it about food on a stick that appeals to the child in us—not to mention actual children? Who knows, but it is a hit with the youngsters. Pick up some paper lollipop sticks at your candymaking source to transform chocolates into pops.

.

Ring around the finger

ROUND SCRUBBY SOAP

MATERIALS

clear glycerin

soap glitter (we used a blend of gold and red)

soap fragrance

soap mold

rings for embedding (twist your own out of craft wire or buy toy rings or faux wedding ring decorations)

round wood or paper box

clear bags or plastic wrap

wire

decorative paper

glue stick

scissors or craft knife

double boiler or microwave

measuring cup

Come clean. Please. These sudsy favors are a gift for the home of friends and family. They are also a whimsical reference to starting with a clean slate and a new beginning. It's easy to incorporate a theme, such as a decorative element you are using elsewhere (like fish, the sign of good luck in many cultures). Or, you can give a matrimonial wink and embed toy rings in the soap that recall the new ones on your finger.

DIRECTIONS

1. Melt chunks of clear glycerin in double boiler or microwave (follow directions on package). Note the capacity of your mold and use a bit more than you will need to fill the molds.

2. Add a one pinch of glitter per soap, 3 to 6 fragrance drops. Refrain from stirring; swirl the soap gently so as not to create too many bubbles or froth.

3. Pour melted soap in measuring cup, then into mold cavities. Stop halfway through the pour and place the rings in the mold. Finish pouring the melted soap into the mold (gently, so as not to disturb the rings).

4. Tap mold to get rid of air bubbles. Let cool completely (1 to 2 hours) then pop out of the mold.

5. For packaging, wrap soap in plastic. Use a glue stick to cover a round box with very sheer decorative paper; let the paper drape naturally then smooth it down. Wrap some wire around the box and twist the ends in a "knot."

VARIATIONS

Make the soaps colorful. Add just a few drops of colorant and the misty translucency of the glycerin soap will remain. Mold them into a variety of shapes.

TIP *Always wrap glycerin soap in plastic first because it is very soft and will smear.*

Anniversary Bonsai

MINIATURE TREE STARTER KIT

Bonsai are miniature trees trimmed and cultivated in small pots to grow in interesting shapes and in miniature form. They require care and can live for a very long time. Visit some botanical gardens that have a bonsai section and you will see some well over one hundred years old. Give guests a starter kit (that is mess free, to boot). The long-growing gift is a symbol of longevity and care.

DIRECTIONS

1. Cut a piece of decorative paper to wrap around the box, and glue it to the exterior.

2. Nestle peat pellet in bonsai pot and place it in box; pack moss around pot.

3. To make miniseed pack: Cut a small rectangle of paper and fold into thirds. Fold one end over middle third, and glue long edges together. Fold other end over and trim to create envelope flap. Place three to five seeds inside. Make a "seeds" label on a piece of contrasting paper and glue it to the front of the pack.

4. To make directions to include: Fold a piece of paper in half. Trace circular object so that side of circle aligns with folded edge. Cut around traced line, leaving the folded edge that aligns with the side of the circle. You now have a circular card in which to include instructions. Include the following points in the instructions: "To use peat pellet, first moisten in pot; then place one or two seeds in peat; keep moist. When the plant outgrows pot, transplant into a larger pot or outdoors."

5. Make name tag out of coordinating paper and punch $1/8$" (0.3 cm) hole in one end. You can also include the name of the tree seeds on the tag.

6. Place directions and seeds inside box and close.

7. Wrap floral wire around box and twist tightly at top; thread name tag on wire; curl ends of wire around pencil.

NOTE *Sizes will be determined by the pot you choose.*

MATERIALS

miniature bonsai pots or
other small ceramic pots

tree seeds

dry peat pellets
(for seed starting)

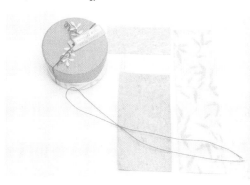

kraft paper boxes

moss

cloth-covered floral wire

assorted papers

pencil or pen

glue stick

scissors or craft knife

$1/8$" (0.3 cm) hole punch
(optional)

Forever Etched in Memory

FROSTED GLASSWARE

MATERIALS

glasses

coordinating beads

silver-colored wire,
20 gauge and 34 gauge

adhesive vinyl

Etchall glass etching
crème

small paintbrush

hole punches (We used
star $^1/_4$" (0.5cm),
$^1/_8$" (0.3 cm) circle,
and a crescent)

round-nosed pliers

rubber gloves

metal-rimmed
vellum tags

fine point pen

Gone are the typical frosted wine and champagne glasses. We like the idea, though, of etched glasses. The permanence of glass etched with a design transforms the ordinary into intriguing. What better occasion to toast to the future than a wedding celebration? Lift these colorful cordial glasses in honor of the happy couple (or in honor of the attending guests as any good host would do) and the etching takes on a different tone. Rather than proper and fussy, these glasses look useful and well crafted, in the vein of the everyday art of the Arts and Crafts movement.

TIP *Cut the vinyl into small pieces when working on a curved surface so that it doesn't wrinkle.*

(fig. 1)

DIRECTIONS

ETCH THE GLASS

1. Punch a design into the adhesive vinyl (*see fig. 1*). Punches come in various designs, so you can personalize the design very easily and quickly.

2. Wash and dry the glass with a lint-free rag. Try not to get any fingerprints on the areas of the glass to be etched.

3. Apply the vinyl pattern to the glass and press it firmly in place.

4. Following the manufacturer's directions, apply a thick even layer of crème to the glass using a small brush. Wait 5 minutes, then rinse the glass off under warm running water and remove the vinyl pattern. Be sure to wear rubber gloves when working with etching crème.

MAKE THE WIRE NAME TAGS

1. Cut off about 6" (15 cm) of 20 gauge wire and about 7" (18 cm) of 34 gauge wire. Begin wrapping the 34 gauge loosely around the 20 gauge.

2. Slip the name tag and bead on the wire. Be sure to select a bead that has a large enough hole to fit around the wire.

3. Curl one end of the wire around a few times using round-nosed pliers, and press the spiral up to keep the bead and tag in place (*see fig. 2*). To create the name tag that fits over the edge of a glass, simply bend it over the edge of the glass and press in place; then curl the other end into a spiral to finish. To create a tag that fits around the base of the glass, follow the instructions above but wrap it around the base of the glass rather than over the edge. To finish, bend the wire to make a hook for closing.

(fig. 2)

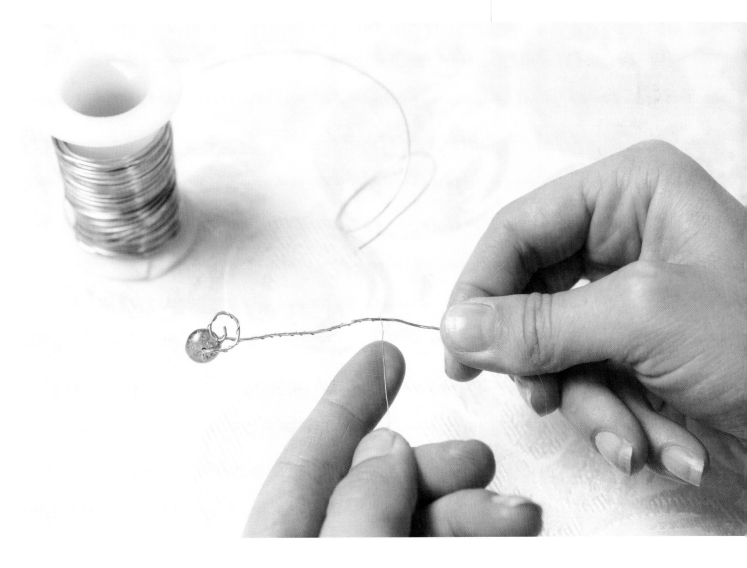

Reflections of Love

MINIMIRROR FAVOR

MATERIALS

Krylon's Looking Glass Base Coat Mirror Paint and Clear Coat Sealer or other spray-mirror product

newspaper (to protect work surface from spray paint)

small squares of glass (approximately 2" × 2" (5 cm × 5 cm)

template from page 296

blue vellum and paper cutouts

glue stick

circular stickers or shelf lining paper cut into shapes (for masking)

silvered copper tape

self-adhesive magnetic strips

Many favors are comestible. Guests eat chocolates, cakes, and candies as they drive home after the festivities, for breakfast the next morning when they wake up late, or for a midnight snack. Some favors do away with food in exchange for a little art. This keepsake favor is a little unusual because it recalls the wedding but without the need for names and dates. A further deviation from the norm is the unique construction of the project—the mirror finish is sprayed on. Carefully lifting a heart shape (or floral shape) from the mirror makes a unique reminder of the event.

DIRECTIONS

1. Cut out templates from adhesive paper, using the shapes from page 296, or create your own. Clean the surface of the glass squares very well and apply adhesive templates onto the glass.

TIP Mirror spray takes a little finesse to work with. Experiment a few times before committing yourself to the project. Make sure the glass is very clean and peel the stencils off carefully.

(fig. 1)

2. Place the prepared glass on newsprint with the stencils facing up. Working in a well-ventilated area, coat the glass with several thin layers of mirror paint and let dry 15 minutes. Coat the painted surface with the sealer following the product instructions and carefully remove the stencil. Let dry. *(see fig. 1)*

3. Turn over the glass so the mirrored area shows through from the back. Cut vellum to size and affix a paper motif to its center. Sandwich the paper between two pieces of glass so that the motif shows through the clear area of the mirrored glass. *(see fig. 2)*

4. Seal the edges of the glass with silvered copper tape and affix thin magnetic strips to the back.

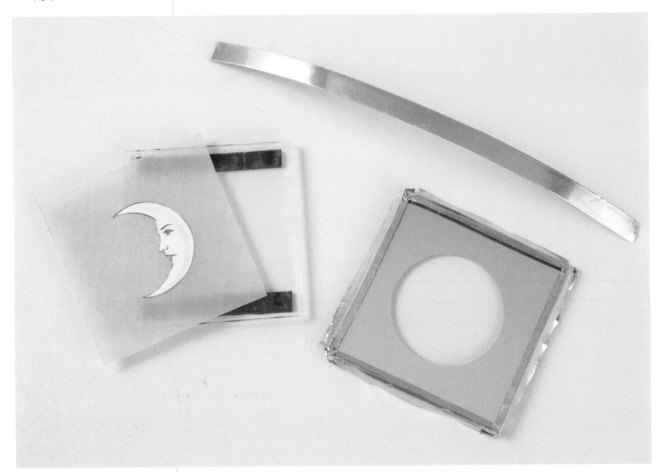

(fig. 2)

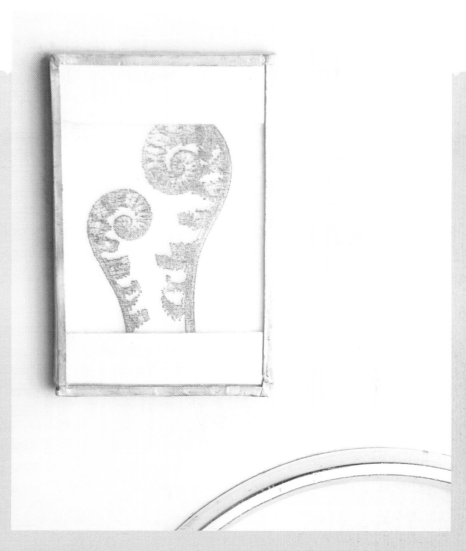

VARIATIONS

• Sandwich a photocopy on acetate between the mirrored glass (we used an image of two ferns). For a diffused effect, gently abrade the back of the acetate with steel wool before inserting the image.

• You can use a different shape if hearts are too standard for you. Go floral with a rounded petal shape or block off a word with stickers for a mirror that really says something.

• Krylon also makes a frosted spray, so you can mirror an entire piece of glass and use a stencil on the front side of the glass to block off a frosted image.

Henna Party

MENDHI KIT

All over the world, women decorate themselves as part of the wedding ritual. Your most familiar form of decoration might be a veil and an up-do—or a manicure. Mendhi application on hands and feet is a common wedding preparation in India. It uses the same process as a henna tattoo that you might see available in some salons and stores—the henna is a plant derivative that temporarily dyes the skin for up to a few weeks. The traditional patterns are lovely and intricate. This kit is the perfect reference to wedding traditions and is also thoroughly modern. Make the kit as a favor for a wedding shower. But, because the dye lasts for a few weeks, make sure that no one in the wedding ceremony uses the kit without knowing fully that it will last. If you are inspired by the henna idea and want to incorporate that tradition into your wedding, visit a professional salon that routinely applies Mendhi patterns and go to your wedding with a little more tradition and filigree.

DIRECTIONS

1. Cut the cardboard into a square measuring 10" × 10" (25 cm × 25 cm) and score two lines down the center of the square to create a "spine." Cut the yellow card stock to fit inside the cardboard "book" and glue with PVA.

2. Layer two rectangles of hand-made paper on top of the yellow card stock. Cut a rectangle of yellow card stock and glue to the front cover. Layer with origami mesh paper and a paisley design cut from vellum. (See the template on pages 296–297 or use clip art.)

3. Place vellum on top of the templates (see pages 296–297) and trace the Mendhi patterns. Fill three glassine envelopes with henna, tea, and some Mendhi designs.

4. Create a small booklet from card stock and vellum in which you explain the process of applying henna designs. Affix all four pieces with clear photo corners to the inside of the kit.

MATERIALS

henna

loose tea

templates from pages 296–297

decorative cardboard

yellow ochre card stock

rice paper, origami mesh and vellum

glassine envelopes

clear photo corners

glue stick

craft glue

scissors

craft knife and cutting mat

felt tipped pen

raffia

circular tags

string

PVA adhesive

See page 296–297 for these templates

MEHNDI DIRECTIONS TO INCLUDE IN KIT

1. Brew the tea and add to the henna powder until it forms a mudlike paste. Add lemon juice and olive oil and let sit for at least 1 hour (overnight is best).

2. Wash skin and apply the henna paste with a fine stick (such as a toothpick) making sure only a thin line of henna touches the skin, not the end of the stick.

3. Let dry several hours and apply lemon juice to moisten the henna as it sets. When the henna has turned a deep red color, carefully scrape off the paste, rub the skin with olive oil, and rinse the area with water. Avoid using soap to prolong the design, which will last for about 2 weeks.

4. For design inspiration, see *Traditional Mehndi Designs: A Treasury of Henna Body Art* by Dorine van den Beukel.

First Impressions

MATERIALS

paperclay (or self-drying clay)

basswood for frame (or an unfinished wood frame)

spackle

acrylic paints

metallic wax (We used silver Rub 'n Buff Wax.)

craft glue (such as Sobo or Tacky Glue)

glass

brushes

craft knife

rolling pin (or cylindrical bottle)

sandpaper

objects to imprint in clay

cardboard, cut to the same size as the frame.

Friends are great collaborators—when you're up to no good (Who skipped college classes with you in favor of a road trip to Niagara Falls?)—and when you want to make something nice. This project calls on everyone's innate ability to read into symbols and make something while talking and laughing. It's a great shower project, so show it to the party organizer . . . or make it at the next night-in with the group. Each of your friends at the party can be in charge of a tile, bringing with them an object that signifies some aspect of marriage, or a memoir of your relationship with your sweetheart. The object does not need to be literal, and only you and your friends might know what the imprint of your cell phone means. This project will not interrupt the talking and frolicking.

(fig. 1)

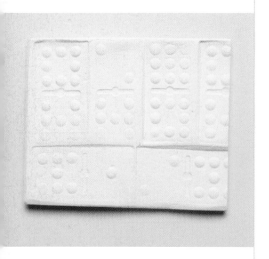

(fig. 2)

DIRECTIONS

1. Build a frame from basswood (or use an unfinished wood frame) and coat it with spackle. Let dry and sand smooth before staining with diluted acrylic paints *(see fig. 1))*. The spackle gives the effect of grout when the tiles are applied on top.

2. Measure your frame to decide the dimensions of the tiles. Flatten the paperclay with a rolling pin to desired thickness and cut with a craft knife to create tiles *(see fig. 2)*.

3. Press found objects into the clay, smooth the edges, and let dry.

4. Paint the tiles with acrylics and let dry. Then rub metallic wax on the tiles to create an aged effect *(see fig. 3)*.

5. Glue the tiles to the frame and let dry. Insert glass, photo, and cardboard backing into the finished frame.

(fig. 3)

Sleeping Beauties

SILKY SLEEP MASK

We all know that planning a wedding can take a lot of energy (although, we sincerely hope that you don't overtax yourself). Even the smallest exertion can rightfully require a renewed habit of napping. We think it's a good idea: Keep your mood high, your energy at top peak, and your skin glowing (extra sleep really does help). Mellow out in style with these silk eye masks. Make a set for your entire bridal party. Better yet, make them at a shower or get-together—each person can make one for someone else. And don't forget the gents. They can use a little snazzy shut-eye as well. Maybe without flowers—or maybe with them.

MATERIALS

dupione silk

silk flowers

flax seed

silk ribbon

fabric glue

scissors

wire cutters

needle and thread

DIRECTIONS

1. Cut out two rectangles of dupione silk measuring approximately 4" × 11" (10 cm × 28 cm). With the silk's right side facing up, apply fabric glue to three edges of one of the rectangles. Place the right side of the second rectangle on top and press the glued seams with your fingers.

2. Trim silk flowers from their stems with wire cutters. After the glue on the rectangle's seams is dry, turn the fabric right side out. Arrange the petals on the silk, affix with a dot of fabric glue and let dry.

3. Use a running stitch to sew a ribbon on each end of the rectangle. Fill the open end of the mask with flax seed and seal the end seam with more fabric glue.

VARIATION

Use loose silk petals trapped under netting instead of gluing the flowers in a specific pattern.

Portable Breeze
COLORFUL FAN

Summer is a popular wedding season. That means blue skies, gorgeous flowers, and heat. The stagnant air that we blissfully pretend to ignore can transform the most well-turned-out wedding guest into a puddle before the vows are even uttered—especially if the wedding is outdoors. Arm guests with a little air-conditioning and fill the gathering with a uniform color. It's dual purposed: coolant and decoration. Imagine a field of friends, fluttering vibrant hand-printed paper—a field of happy, cool people.

DIRECTIONS

1. Enlarge and trace the template on page 298 onto the card stock and the decorative paper. Cut out two shapes from the card stock and one shape from the decorative paper.

2. Apply hot-melt glue to half of the handle and press firmly onto one card stock cut-out, making sure it is centered.

3. Spray the decorative paper with spray adhesive, in a well-ventilated area (or outdoors). Line up the decorative paper with the second card stock cut-out and press firmly together, pressing out all the air bubbles.

4. Use spray adhesive to join the two halves of the fan together. Line up the edges carefully. The decorative paper should face out (obviously), and the handle should be sandwiched between fan layers. Press firmly to assure a good contact between the paper.

5. Trim any uneven edges. Punch a small hole on each side of the handle at the base of the fan. Thread the ribbon through and tie.

TIP *If an outdoor wedding is in your plans, remind people on the invitation to wear a hat. Not only are hats a marvelous wedding standard, they will protect people from the harsh sun.*

MATERIALS

card stock paper

template from page 298

coordinating decorative paper

tongue depressors, or specially made balsa handles from the craft store

hot-melt glue gun

spray mount

scissors

$1/4$" (0.5cm) holepunch

ribbon

VARIATION

You can run the card stock through the printer before you cut out the shield shape. Print your names and the date or a quote or image.

VARIATION

The shield shape seems to catch the air very well, but other shapes are suitable, too. Circles can look neat (and are easy to cut out with a compass cutter). You can even scan in a leaf into your computer, lighten the color, print it out onto light green paper and make leaf fans for everyone.

Swirly Container

INTERLOCKING PETAL BOX

These little boxes were inspired by a chocolate that arrived in a similar, but stouter, box. The chocolate was good, but the box was fabulous. The interlocking tabs are petal-like, making the box a perfect container for wildflower seeds. Of course, the boxes could hold candied almonds, sweets, rose petals, or any number of other things.

MATERIALS

card stock paper

template from page 298

decorative paper

scissors

pencil

spray adhesive

straight edge

bone folder

4" (10 cm) circle of tulle

ribbon

wildflower seeds or lavender flowers

color printer

VARIATION

Consider filling the box with rose petals to be tossed as confetti during the evening, or with candy-coated chocolate, without the need for a tuille bag. Instead of making your own tuille gather, you could purchase premade tuille bags in many different colors at craft stores.

DIRECTIONS

1. Using the template on page 298, trace the box shape onto card stock paper and decorative paper. Cut out the shapes.

2. Use spray adhesive to glue the card stock and decorative paper shapes together. Take care to line up the shapes and have "right sides" facing outward (there usually is no right side to card stock, though). Press firmly and use the edge of a bone folder to force out any air bubbles.

3. Line up the straight edge along the fold lines and score the line with the tip of the bone folder. Fold the flaps of the box up along the score lines.

4. Prepare the box contents. You can put candies or petals directly in the box. Or, gather candies or wildflower seeds in a circle of tuille and tie the small bundle closed with a ribbon. Put the bundle inside the box and interlock the swirly flaps to close the box.

TIP *If printing out a message that lines up with the bottom of the box is too much hassle, print a sheet of "bottoms," cut them out, and glue them into the box bottoms.*

Wintery Topiary

BEADED PLACE CARD HOLDER

Place cards can range anywhere from a simple piece of paper to a river pebble with a name written across it to a portable *objet d'art*. This place card adds some glamour to the glimmering lights. Crown each place setting with a beaded topiary and guests will know where they sit in style. The small tree will shimmer in the candlelight as the white and teal beads catch the light. The colors are particularly appropriate for a winter wedding.

MATERIALS

styrofoam ball

small terra-cotta pot

thin dowel (for stem)

florist's foam

strung beads

micro beads

metallic paper

organza ribbon

craft glue

acrylic paints

metallic wax (We used Rub 'n Buff.)

cloth or fine steel wool

vellum

wire

DIRECTIONS

1. Paint the terra-cotta pot, dowel, and Styrofoam ball in a color that coordinates with your table setting (we used various shades of turquoise with silvery metallics) and set aside to dry. Rub metallic wax over the painted pot and burnish with a soft cloth.

2. Insert florist's foam into the pot and then glue a circle of decorative paper to the top of the foam. Leaving 1" (3 cm) bare on each end of the dowel, brush it with craft glue and wind with strung beads.

3. Brush the top 1" (3 cm) of the beaded "stem" with glue and push into the Styrofoam ball. Apply craft glue to the painted ball and sprinkle with micro beads. Push the topiary into the florist's foam and allow to dry.

4. Embellish the pot with organza ribbon and a vellum place card.

VARIATION
MATERIALS

bay leaves

**paper fern leaves (at a
paper or craft store)**

styrofoam ball

twig

small terra-cotta pot

moss

florist's foam

ribbon

card stock

**alphabet stamps and
ink pad**

acrylic paints

hot-melt glue gun

sandpaper

bronze gel pen

VARIATION

*You can also evoke the
Tuscan hillsides, aromatic
food, and wonderful glasses
of Montepulciano. The
relaxed, sun-soaked feeling
of this terra-cotta version
will enhance any robust,
festive, and rustic reception.
Depending on the materials
used, guests may enjoy a
lingering scent of the hills
outside of Florence for
weeks to come.*

DIRECTIONS

1. Cut a twig to the appropriate length for your topiary and poke a hole in the base
   of a Styrofoam ball. Hot glue bay leaves and paper ferns to the ball and set aside.

2. Paint the twig with metallic acrylic paint and inject hot glue into the hole at the
   ball's base.

3. Paint the terra-cotta pot with antique white acrylic paint, let dry, and sand to distress the finish.

4. Push florist's foam into the pot and glue the twig and ball structure into the foam. Finish
   with a layer of moss, wire ribbon, and a name tag with hand-stamped letters.

PLACE CARD IDEAS

Sign in Here

MATERIALS

blank "memory" books

decorative papers:
blue and white vellum,
blue and white Japanese
lace paper

white tulle

antique, lowercase
alphabet stamp set

black ink pad
(to coordinate with
black wire binding)

scissors or craft knife

glue stick

colored pencils and
other art supplies

scallop paper edgers
(optional)

It is kind of silly for guests to stand in line as they enter a reception, waiting to sign their names in the small space allotted in the guest book. Or should guests remember to leave their dinner companions and sign the book, midparty? Aren't we all tempted to take up more than a single line, anyway? Give each table a couple of miniature guest books instead. Guests can write, draw, and share their stories about the bride and groom in each book, bride stories in "she" and groom tales in "he." After the event, the bride and groom can read all the books and share all their great stories (that they might not have shared yet). Enhance the creativity quotient and stash pens, pencils, crayons, and Polaroid iZone cameras with sticky film on each table.

DIRECTIONS

1. Stamp "he" on lower right corner of a book and "she" on the other. Let dry. Ink on vellum takes longer to dry than it does on regular paper.

2. Place a square of blue vellum over the "he" stamping, then top with a smaller square of blue lace paper. Place a piece of tulle over the "she" stamping and top with a smaller square of white lace paper. Use a glue stick and small dabs in the corners of the materials to secure; any more will be too much for thin, delicate papers and fabric, and would cause the vellum to wrinkle.

3. Bundle pencils together and wrap with a piece of vellum. Use glue to seal. We trimmed the vellum with scallop paper edgers.

DIRECTIONS

1. Stamp "he" on lower right corner of a book and "she" on the other. Let dry. Ink on vellum takes longer to dry than it does on regular paper.

2. Place a square of blue vellum over the "he" stamping, then top with a smaller square of blue lace paper. Place a piece of tulle over the "she" stamping and top with a smaller square of white lace paper. Use a glue stick and small dabs in the corners of the materials to secure; any more will be too much for thin, delicate papers and fabric, and would cause the vellum to wrinkle.

3. Bundle pencils together and wrap with a piece of vellum. Use glue to seal. We trimmed the vellum with scallop paper edgers.

VARIATION

A larger book means more room to draw. Stamp "guests" on a piece of torn paper and layer it over handmade paper. Add a fiber border and a fiber place marker. Cover a can with decorative paper and tie with a fiber that matches the book's place marker. Fill the can with writing supplies.

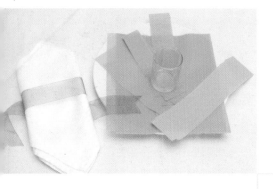

Underwater Hurricane

SWIRLY BLUE CANDLEHOLDERS

MATERIALS

**Mod Podge
(or decoupage medium
or collage glue)**

foam brush

tissue paper

**stamps (We used
Stampendous! Perfectly
Clear Stamps; the set is
called Maggie's Daisy and
includes both stamps;
product number SSC002.)**

**stamp ink pad (We used a
Kaleidacolor Raised
Rainbow Dye Inkpad
by Tsukineko; the
color scheme is "Blue
Breeze" and there are
five color variations.)**

glass vase and votives

Candlelight does wonders for ambiance. The flicker of candles adds a fire and sparkle to both eyes and moods, and everyone looks phenomenal with the soft, ever-changing light. Enhance that trend by decorating tables with these large lanterns and miniature votives. Each table will be swimming in a shimmering blue, a mix of campfire, romantic dinner, and the deep sky.

VARIATION

Consider a warm alternate to the color palette: Cover rounded glass votives with tangerine-colored tissue. Use delicate dried flowers as a substitute for stamped design accents. In our version, we created a slightly darker background for the flower using a more intense shade of tissue. After the tissue layer is completely dry, add a drop of glue, then gently press the flower onto the surface and smooth it out. Once that dries, coat the entire flower with a layer of Mod Podge or other decoupage medium to protect it.

(fig. 1)

1. Use a ruler to tear tissue into strips of different widths; trap the tissue underneath the ruler, and pull up on one side. This will give you a straight, even tear *(see fig. 1)*.

2. Brush Mod Podge on the vase or on a votive; lay a strip of tissue on top, making sure it is fairly straight. Smooth the strip down with the brush; use additional Mod Podge if neces sary. Continue layering strips until you are happy with the level of transparency (three lay ers works well). **N O T E:** Strips do not have to be perfectly sized before applying them; you can tear off the top and bottom once the Mod Podge has set—then you will have a bit of an edge to smooth over the top and bottom edges of the glass.

(fig. 2)

3. Stamp some strips with the flower motif. When dry, adhere to the vase and votives.
   NOTE: The stamp pad we used goes from light to dark blue; so for some of the flower stamping we used two or three different colors at once. For the smaller stamp we used one color per stamping *(see fig. 2)*.

4. Stamp the swirl directly on the vases and votives when the Mod Podge is dry.

Flowers for Everyone

MATERIALS

4 square vases

green bamboo

white waterlilly dahlia

river stones

water

sharp knife

Flower styling is more of an art than a craft. You need to see the end result in your head before starting and sculpt the arrangement into being as you go. If you've got the hang of it, flower arranging can be a great and innovative way to add your spark to the surroundings (besides with your dazzling self). It is fairly common to see large bundles of flowers in pinks, purples, and whites do duty as a table centerpiece. Because you've already seen that a million times, we feel you can probably pull it off already. We want to show you some different paths that an arrangement can take.

Flowers are also a great way to bridge the sometimes formidable distance between traditional and supermodern. Really, that distance is not so great—so many of us have facets in both domains. Those traits, attitudes, and tendencies combine well into a personality, but still, it can be difficult to put that same balance into action in a big event, when you need it the most. A bundle of traditional flowers (favorites through the ages) can soften the hard lines and colors of a modern setting, whether it's the modern architecture of a church, or your grandparents' Frank Lloyd Wright Usonian. By the same token, sleek, elegant

1. Cut the bamboo into equal lengths that just fit into the square vases, lying down.

2. Fill each vase differently. One vase can be filled entirely with bamboo. Another can be partially filled with bamboo and topped with a single white flower. Others can include river stones and any other simple combination of basic materials.

flower arrangements that rely on strong lines and shape will do wonders to modernize the historic home that the reception is set in. We are not suggesting that you use modern flower arrangements to mask the filigreed crown molding. If you try to do that, the design elements will not build on each other but, rather, look unpaired. With the right balance of styles, you can enhance both the traditional and contemporary. Do a little experimentation along the lines of *Homefront in the Garden* (from the BBC) and apply their concept of supermodern meets ordinary flowers, because it can work vice-versa as well. We are even particularly fond of a haphazard bundle of wildflowers in a watering can if the setting is right.

Typically, a bride has a bouquet (but not always—you could just carry a purse, or nothing at all), the groom has a boutonniere, the wedding party has their respective flowers, and then there are decorative flowers for the wedding and reception sites. Take a swatch of the dress fabric to the florist and match some of the flowers for the boutonniere to that color. Do so even if it's a white dress, because there are so many varieties of white; it could be anything from snow, eggshell, pearl, glacier, bone, or even cloud—some are more yellow than others and you don't want a flower to make the dress look dingy. Even if none of the other flowers match a certain color scheme, the two of you will "match" if the boutonniere coordinates with the dress.

For the reception space, keep in mind that a table's center-piece rests between one guest trying to have a conversation with another on the opposite side of the table. A gorgeous 3-foot (91 cm)-tall bundle of assorted garden delights can be a serious hindrance to an otherwise brilliant conversation if people cannot maintain eye contact without getting a kink in the neck. The solution may be small vases. Sure, on a table that seats eight people, a 4-inch (10 cm)-tall vase can look dinky. It won't look undersized at all, though, if you use four of them together as a single centerpiece. These square vases hold chopped bamboo in a most unusual way—more as terrain than cut flower. Arranging each square of the centerpiece in a slightly different way adds texture and variety to the table and allows people a field of garden goodness without the need to peer through foliage.

Is it the vase or the champagne that makes things teeter? Roly vases are part decoration and part game. Create a triad of gerbera daisies in the middle of the table and watch guests play with the vases.

VARIATION

Height doesn't have to be an enemy. A moderately tall vase is easy to manage. And simple arrangements of a single type of flower are the easiest for you to pull off. Bundle a thick handful of calla lilies, holding them in place with clear hair elastics. Trim the bottoms so they are flat and even. Rest the bottoms of the calla lilies on the table and ease the bundle off to the side, titling the bundle with the bottoms still resting on the table. The stems remain parallel to each other but each flower is visible in a kind of upright cascade. Cut the bottoms even to the right length and stand in a thin vase.

Diversions Add Texture

AN OCCUPIED GUEST IS A HAPPY GUEST

Hosting a wedding comprises a lot of little things. A meaningful ceremony paired with a party sounds simple enough, and it can be, but some elements can transform a good host into a great one. Try throwing an event that matches your style and personality and puts the guests at ease, whether it's a barbeque or a black tie affair. The other is

providing guests with a balance of activities that allows them to look after themselves. After all, you can't watch over them at every moment of the day.

The surest way to keep guests active and happy, without additional attention, is to creatively mix guests together. You are hip and fascinating, and chances are a good percentage of your guests are, too. The wallflowers are fascinating, too, and they will get drawn into conversations by your friends with an ample supply of aplomb. Planning seating arrangements can be taxing, but getting together a mix of potential conversationalists is part of the fun. (Katie is a chemist, and so is Michael. Michael's wife is studying to be a master sommelier, and Jared loves to eat out—perfect!). People of the same age do not automatically have common interests, so consider personality more than generational guides. Young and old may like the same things and have an amazing time together. Don't let age be the stringent rule for seating.

But aside from riveting conversation, what more can be done to keep people happy? There is dinner, which in our circles always keeps the conversation going and going and going. There is also dancing, which keeps a party roaring. But not all activity needs to be major. Sometimes, the small filler bits provide enough play to help transition between activities and keep the party moving. What to do when there is a lull in the conversation, or when the photos have gone on forty minutes longer than planned, or when dancers need a break and sit back down at a semiempty table? Provide "fidget toys." Those are items that don't take a lot of concentration but provide a minute or two of diversion while striking up a new conversation. Things like pinball boxes with ball-bearings, spinning tops that coordinate with the décor, fortune-tellers (remember those folded-paper toys?) that are filled with romantic questions or "predictions."

Some weddings are a reunion of far-flung friends and family that have shared your world-wide adventures. It is possible that there will be tables where few people know each other. Help them find conversation by including a little icebreaker. Include a list of adventures that you have shared with people at the table as a way to make their introductions easier. The person the groom backpacked across Norway with might not introduce himself that way, so a little hint ensures that the conversation kicks off to a great start. If there are only a few tables filled with strangers, you have a choice as good hosts: rush to those tables first to make effusive introductions or, better yet, arm some of the outgoing friends at each table with a little history beforehand. That way, the conversation will start with "So, Alice tells me you're an astronaut," or "What was it like cooking for the president of France?" It will take off from there.

If the event is complicated (and even some easy-to-put-together ones are), you can print up programs for each place setting. If dancing is a major part of your vision, you can hint for guests to hit the dance floor with a program decorated with dance-step instructions.

Whatever the situation, if you supply guests with their basic needs for enjoyment—food, drink, and conversation—they will pretty much take care of themselves, leaving you time to visit with as many people as possible and enjoy the kick-off to your marriage instead of worrying about whether people are having fun or not.

Wishing Tree

MESSAGE CENTER FOR FOND WISHES

We like the idea of fêting a couple and their new marriage with everyone's best wishes. Sure, we wish people well all the time, but this occasion calls for a little extra demonstration of our hopes for their future. Set a collection of curly willow branches somewhere at the reception next to a stack of vellum leaves and a pen. People will take the time to write a short message to the couple, a wish for their future, or a piece of wisdom they want to share. As the evening progresses, the tree will fill with leaves that flutter as people walk or dance by.

DIRECTIONS

1. Place vellum on top of the templates and trace leaf shapes (or invent your own). Cut out the leaves and punch a W " (0.5 cm) -hole at the base of each. Insert an eyelet in each hole and affix with an eyelet tool and hammer.

2. Thread 4" (10 cm) of fine wire through each eyelet and twist to secure.

3. Push curly willow into florist's foam, insert in a planter, and layer moss on top of the foam. Tie three layers of organdy ribbon around the planter (or use dyed raffia for a more rustic effect). Have the leaves and metallic pens ready next to the wish tree for guests to write on as they arrive. Attach the leaves to the branches with the wire.

MATERIALS

curly willow

vellum

planter

ribbon

hole punch (We used W " (0.5 cm))

eyelets and eyelet tool

florist's wire

florist's foam

dried moss

metallic gel pens

wire cutters

scissors

leaf images templates (see page 299)

Fortune Cache

MATERIALS

matchboxes

assorted handmade
papers

charms

beads (for "feet" on
bottom of boxes)

Sobo craft glue

E6000 silicone glue (for
attaching charms and
beads)

gel pen

embroidery thread

Opening things gives everyone a thrill. It doesn't matter what it is, we love to reveal the hidden goodies. The joy of it never leaves us—that's the key to exciting gifts and direct-mail offers. Guests sit down to this miniature chest made from a decoupaged matchbox that is set on a platform of wire and beads. No one but the most fatigued or disenchanted could resist opening it up to see what is inside. Place a little fortune or well-wishes inside to reward their eternal and sprightly curiosity. The treasure could be a message from you and your sweetheart, a pebble with a word on it, or a small, emblematic object for them to keep in their pockets.

DIRECTIONS

1. Cut papers to the appropriate sizes for the matchbox's drawer and exterior.

2. Glue papers on the outside and inside of the box. Create a miniature collage on the top of the box by combining a variety of paper textures, patterns, and colors.

3. Attach a charm on top of the collage with the silicone glue and let set. Adhere the bead "feet" in the same manner on the bottom of the box.

4. Write a quote or a fortune for your guest on a piece of the handmade paper, roll up into a scroll, and wrap with embroidery thread. Place the secret message inside the box.

TIP *Consider including a favorite poem rolled on a scroll of paper, a small seashell or keepsake from a recent trip, a pressed leaf, seeds for a plant that you love, or a list of other historic occasions that occurred on the same date as your wedding.*

Kids Are Guests, Too

HOW TO ENTERTAIN YOUR SMALL CELEBRANTS

We're firm believers that it's OK to be a kid. So often kids are placed in situations where they have to act grown-up, sit still, and be quiet. That doesn't seem so fair when they haven't developed the skills that let them do that for hours on end. (Frankly, there are adults that haven't developed that skill either.) If you are including the kids on your guest list, be kind to them and give them some tools to have an enjoyable day, too.

The smallest children really want attention. And at a wedding there are often plenty of adults and family members that are happy to cuddle and hold the young niece they hardly ever see. The older children are, however, the more they need something beyond time sitting on Aunt Florence's lap.

BOREDOM IS THE ENEMY

Parents of unhappy kids are unhappy guests. They feel tired and annoyed and unable to fully enjoy the celebration. But kids shouldn't be made to sit on their hands just to keep their parents happy. That's unrealistic and not that nice. Instead, remember that the reception is a party for everyone, young and old, and give the younger set the chance to revel in their vices as well (OK, playing with toys and eating candy doesn't yet qualify as a vice, but you get our meaning).

FOOD

Many an otherwise happy kid was rendered miserable by elaborate food that is overwhelming to their palates. Discuss food options ahead of time with parents if you're concerned. Arrange a tray of PB&Js, chips, and other standard goodies that kids can retreat to if they can't handle the farfalle with foie gras and truffle oil . . . or the chicken. Even if they've cried "finished!" after three bites of the grown-up meal, they may get peckish again before the party's over. Keeping kid-friendly food handy is never a mistake.

THE "HARD STUFF"

Many parents try to keep the kids away from sweets, but the adults are living it up, and the kids should be allowed to, too. Dole out the sweets in a fun way. Create a tray with small bundles of goodies. The small packages will mitigate the tummy-aches (maybe) and allow kids to have a container all to themselves. Wrap three licorice ropes with a fourth for a sweet bundle. Make small "bags" out of colorful paper and fill with small candies like M&Ms or miniature candy bars.

PLAYTIME

Kids will run around, dance up a storm, and play with other young guests. But if there won't be more than a couple kids, offer up some play materials to keep the young set happy and entertained. Cars and trucks are perfect tabletop entertainment for boys and girls. Driving a fire truck along the table can keep a child enthralled in make-believe land for a while. And what more perfect kid-themed favor than a new toy? For those in prime dress-up age, you can include some hats like old ladies wore to tea ages ago, tiaras, cowboy hats, or sheriff badges. You don't want to turn the reception into a circus, but two or three kids running around hardly makes a circus. Or save the dress-up goods for a relaxed rehearsal dinner.

Never underestimate the power of crayons, colored pencils, and paper to amuse kids and keep them in high spirits (forget about the markers . . . you don't want them around dress-up clothes).

WHERE TO PUT IT ALL

You don't want the kids' diversions to dominate or distract others, but a little planning will keep kids and their parents in the mood to celebrate. All you need is a small collection of objects and goodies appropriate for the size of the gathering and the number of kids. You can arrange a small table with the munchies off to the side. The toys can be given directly to the parents for dispensing when the kids get a little antsy.

When you are having a party, you are host to all guests, big and little. A little attention to these smaller participants may not fix all the fussing, but the effort expended is worth it.

Gifts & Goodies

The gifts and goodies that guests and attendants receive are more than mere presents. They are mementos. Although people will appreciate and enjoy the decorations, the food, and the touching elements that you have folded into your wedding, items that guests take with them are tangible reminders of the day's events. It makes sense, then, to imbue them with the same style, humor, and elegance that shape your wedding and your relationships.

In this chapter, we include gifts that can go to shower guests, attendants, or wedding guests. Favors and gifts don't have to be elaborate or expensive, but they should be thoughtful and indicative of the connection between you and the recipients.

Sometimes brides are ambushed with a surprise wedding shower and therefore have nothing to do with the favors. But many women have significant influence over the style and the favors given.

Most gifts in this section are suitable for everyone. Some gifts, though, are best suited for specific people. Whether your wedding will be a small affair or an event covered in *Town and Country*, your tight group of friends helps you along the way. They assist you in deciding between heels or flats, provide distraction when your mother gets too taxing (it's not her fault), fête your future at your shower, and stand up in fancy outfits during the ceremony. These comrades are the only worthy recipients of "Knickers with a Twist" (see page 230), whereas every wedding or shower guest can enjoy the retro ball bearing game (see page 234).

Deciding which gifts to give out is a fun but difficult task. Consider the complexity of the project and the time involvement. The "Field of Flowers" frame (see page 204) is more complex than the "Mooning Over Memories" frame (see page 220), and is therefore much easier to make for a smaller group of people. If you take into account the time you have available, the intricacy of the project, and the recipients, you are sure to delight guests with tokens that remind them of the wonderful time you have had together.

Field of Flowers

PHOTO PEBBLE RESIN FRAME

Resin starts as a rather toxic liquid (Use it outside and keep it away from children and pregnant women, please!), and solidifies into a unique, rock-hard transparent material. Here, glass pebbles are set into a sea of resin, making a weighty and sculptural photo frame. The glass pebbles magnify the words and images beneath them. We pasted flower images under most of the pebbles. Beneath a few others, we pasted words, the names of the bride and groom, and the wedding date in coordinating colors.

1. Take out the glass and backing of the picture frame. Prime the wood with the white primer. Let dry.

2. With your favorite computer layout software, make a document and import your favorite flower photos. Reduce the images until they look like they will fit under each photo pebble. Duplicate the flower images until you have at least seventy. To test the size, print out a low-quality version of the images and place a few different glass pebbles on them, checking that the image is recognizable and doesn't need to be reduced further. The pebbles vary in size, so try several.

3. Find a typeface suitable to your taste and set some text in a size that will fit under the pebbles. Some ideas for words: the couple's names, the wedding date, and romantic words like "love" and "joy." These can be placed in the same document with the flower images.

VARIATION *Keen on the unique frame, but not much of a floral person? Go for modern graphics like bulls-eye patterns in repeating colors, or plain fields of three different colors.*

MATERIALS

5" × 7" (12.7 cm × 17.8 cm) unpainted wood picture frame with 1 1/2" (3.8 cm) wide border

At least seventy photo pebbles

Personal computer

Glossy photo paper that works for laser or inkjet printers

Color printer

Your favorite computer layout software

Stock CD of images of flowers (also available on Photodisc.com)

PVA glue

16 oz. (473 ml) box Envirotex Lite epoxy (resin)

Small paper bowl

Inexpensive 1/2" (1.3 cm) wide paint brush

White or gray tile grout

Craft knife

White primer

White or ivory semigloss interior latex paint

Masking tape

Two packages white polymer clay

Rolling pin

Hairdryer

7" × 9" (17.8 cm × 22.9 cm) or larger cardboard gift box

Goggles and industrial duty rubber gloves

4. Print the document on glossy photo paper. Print enough copies of the document to get the quantity you need for the pebbles. Wait about 5 minutes for the ink to dry.

5. Pour some PVA glue into a paper bowl. Using a paintbrush, paint a small amount of glue evenly onto the back of a pebble and adhere pebble to flower image or word. To avoid smearing the ink, do not wiggle the pebble once it is on the printout. Repeat this process until all of the pebbles have been placed over a flower or word. Let glue set for about 15 minutes.

6. Use the craft knife to cut out the paper around each pebble. Keep the blade as close to the pebble as possible.

7. Arrange all the pebbles on the frame until you get the look and feel you like. We centered the couple's names and the date on the bottom of the frame. Glue the pebbles into place one by one with PVA glue. Let the pebbles dry in place for 2 hours.

8. Run masking tape around the exterior and interior of the frame.

9. Roll out a 7 ½" x 20" (19.1 cm x 50.8 cm) slab of polymer clay. Cut lengthwise into eight strips 2 ½" (6.4 cm) wide. Press the strips of clay around the exterior and interior walls of the frame, forming a clay wall around the interior and exterior, bringing height of clay up to the height of the pebbles.

10. Place frame in cardboard box.

11. Bring project outdoors or to an area with excellent cross-ventilation. **Important: Please wear industrial gloves and goggles.** The resin is highly toxic. Make sure you read the resin package for all instructions, ingredients, and safety guidelines. Follow package directions. Pour the resin into a plastic cup and stir well. Then pour resin into frame, halfway up the pebble height, and let it set for 5 minutes.

12. Use a hairdryer to get all the air bubbles out of the resin. Let resin set for 24 hours.

13. Remove clay walls, then the masking tape. Paint the sides of the frame with one or two coats of the white or ivory paint and let dry. Replace glass, put your favorite photo in, and pop the backing in place.

TIP *If you don't have digital images of flowers, you can cut them out of catalogs or magazines. Try to find images that are similar to each other in style. You can multiply the images by making color photocopies of your favorites.*

When the Party's Over Album

MATERIALS

One sheet colored bristol board or card stock weight paper, at least 30" × 7" (76.2 cm × 17.8 cm)

One 20" × 30" (50.8 cm × 76.2 cm) sheet cream-colored card stock

One sheet decorative paper (hand block printed or wallpaper)

6 $\frac{1}{8}$" (15.6 cm) colored eyelet grommets

1 yard (.9 m) organdy or organza ribbon in coordinating color

One package photo corners

Bone folder

Hammer

Eyelet setting tool

Hole punch

PVA glue

Inexpensive paintbrush

Craft knife

Metal ruler

Sharp pencil

One thumb tack

Drafting triangle

No doubt, your nuptial festivities will rage on into the night. (Here's to that!) Still, at some point, people have to go home—or out for breakfast. When the party's over, keep the action fresh in people's minds with a little photographic help. Instead of making everyone wait for a peek at your encyclopedia-size wedding album (whenever it gets finished), send everyone his or her own miniature album. You can customize each one, so your college housemate receives a photo of himself raising a glass with your cousin June.

1. Cut bristol board to measure 28" x 5" (71.1 cm x 12.7 cm). Fold in half, so the folded product measures 14" x 5" (35.6 cm x 12.7 cm). Score the fold by running a bone folder along it, making it crisp and straight.

2. Unfold the paper. Fold both paper edges inward to meet the center fold. Score the new folds with the bone folder *(see fig. 1)*.

3. Unfold the new folds and cut $\frac{1}{2}$" (1.3 cm) off both edges. These will be the inside flaps of the photo booklet.

4. Refold the booklet. On the front cover, connect the opposing corners, making two pencil lines that form a big "X." The intersection point is the center of the cover *(see fig. 2)*.

5. Measure out 1" (2.5 cm) from the center point in all directions (top, bottom, right, and left) and mark out the 2" (5.1 cm) square in the middle of the cover *(see fig. 3)*.

6. Cut out the square with a craft knife and ruler. Use a triangle to help keep the cut lines squared.

7. Measure and cut a 30" x 7" (76.2 cm x 17.8 cm) piece of decorative paper.

8. Brush a thin layer of PVA glue on the paper.

TIP *Kolo mass produces this type of album. You could simply paste the decorative paper onto the cover and add the grommets and your own decorative ribbon.*

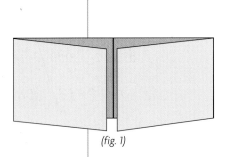

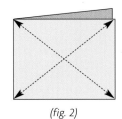

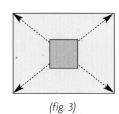

(fig. 1)   *(fig. 2)*   *(fig. 3)*

9. Flatten out the bristol board cover and place in the center of the paper.

10. Smooth out any bumps in the paper with the bone folder. Let the glue dry approximately $\frac{1}{2}$ hour.

11. Using a craft knife, trim decorative paper down to the size of the bristol board.

12. Place the decorative side down on a cutting surface. Cut two diagonals in the square picture window—upper left corner to lower right, and upper right to lower left.

13. Fold back the newly created triangles, score with bone folder and glue to the non-decorative side *(see fig. 4)*.

14. Make the sheets and endpapers of the book by cutting out three 14" x 5" wide (35. 6 cm x 12.7 cm) rectangles of the cream bristol board.

15. Fold each sheet in half and score with bone folder.

16. Unfold the sheets and stack them. Align the sheets and trim off any excess with the craft knife. Place the sheets into the cover.

17. Break two staples from the pack. Do not staple the book with a stapler.

18. Make a small pencil mark on the outside spine of the cover, $\frac{3}{4}$" (1.9 cm) from the top and bottom edge. Measure the width of the staple span and make a pencil mark that distance away from both pencil marks.

19. Using your tack, make a hole at each pencil mark, pushing through all four layers. Take care to keep the papers aligned so the hole passes through the fold line in each of the sheets.

20. Center a favorite picture in the inside front cover, so it shows through the photo window. Hold it in place with a little PVA glue or a small piece of drafting tape.

(fig. 4)   (fig. 5)

21. Brush the inside covers with PVA glue and press the first and last pages onto the inside covers, forming the endpapers. Smooth out any bumps with the bone folder. Take care not to press very hard on the picture window.

22. Place the staples through the holes and pinch the staples shut on the center spread by bearing down on staples with a screwdriver.

23. Make a tick mark 2 ½" (6.4 cm) from the bottom edge and ¼" (6.4 mm) in from the spine on front cover. Make another tick mark 2 ½" (6.4 cm) from the bottom edge and ¼" (6.4 mm) in from right edge on cover. Flip book over and do the same on the back.

24. Using hole punch, make a hole in center of all of the tick marked areas. Then open out front and back flaps.

25. Take an eyelet grommet and place the right side through the front hole. Flip book non-decorative side down and place eyelet setting tool through into the back of the grommet. Hit the tool with a hammer until the grommet begins to flange out to the sides of the hole.

26. Repeat this process through all of the holes, keeping grommets' right sides showing on the decorative side of the cover.

27. Close flaps and run ribbon through grommets as follows: Feed ribbon through right front grommet straight into left inside front cover flap grommet. Run ribbon over right inside front flap out through the front spine grommet. Wrap the ribbon around outside spine. Pull through back right spine grommet, run over the inside back flap and out through the right inside back cover flap grommet, and out through the back cover grommet. Trim edges of ribbon evenly (see fig. 5).

28. Using photo corners, place your favorite wedding photos into book and give to family and friends.

Jordan Bombonière

Candy-coated almonds are a popular and affordable favor. Their symbolism as the union of the sweet and the bitter has helped them endure through generations. But just because millions of people have given them as favors is no reason to avoid them—of course that's no reason to use them, either. If you like the underlying symbolism, by all means make them a small gift for your guests. If you like the idea of sweets for your guests, but you aren't keen on the typical (and tooth-breaking) goodie, use the best-wrapped chocolates you can find instead. The real key is to make your version just a little bit different than everyone else's. The standard is to grab a square of tulle, plop some Jordan almonds inside, gather it up, and tie with a ribbon or (really not our style) a rubber band. Yes, it's easy and, yes, it's what everyone does.

Our version may be a little more complicated, but on the difficulty scale, it still ranks as "able to do when you're brain-dead tired." We used two tones of tulle and small faux flowers to enhance the traditional.

1. Place the cake round over a piece of pink tulle and cut around the shape with scissors. Repeat the process with the green tulle.

2. Place a sheet of the round pink tulle on flat surface, then place the round green tulle on top of it. Place about eleven of the almonds in the center of the tulle.

3. Gather tulle tightly around the almonds, and tie off with a 12" (30.5 cm) length of ribbon. Tie ribbon in a bow then place a single flower in the center of the bow, wrapping wire around package, under the secured ribbon.

4. To finish off the free ends of the ribbon with style, pinch the ends in half length-wise (so the ribbon is narrower). Snip the ribbon with scissors held at a 45°angle. The finished end will look like a pennant tail. Repeat on other free end. Trim top of netting to neaten and finish edges.

TIP *Speaking of symbolism, wrap the candies (almond or others) in odd numbers. Because an odd number cannot be divided evenly in half, it is thought to symbolize the inseparability of the couple.*

MATERIALS

Pink and green tulle or netting

12" (30.5 cm) cardboard cake round

1/2" (1.3 cm) wide green silk ribbon

Packet of paper flowers with wire stem

Jordan almonds, pralined hazelnuts, or other yummies

Scissors

Flower Power Jewelry

BEADED RING, NECKLACE, AND BRACELET

MATERIALS
FOR RING

One small
package
seed beads

Six 4 mm
crystal beads

Six 6 mm
crystal beads

One package
"no stretch" nylon
bead string, size # 4 in
coordinating color

One package of
clear stretchable
bead cord

Five bendable
bead needles
(small enough to
fit through a
seed bead)

Needle-nose pliers

A tiny boutique in Barcelona sells a ring and bracelet similar to these. Never able to leave well enough alone, we came up with an adaptation that we like a little better—and a necklace to match.

The outstanding element of this jewelry is the stylized flower pattern that is not too delicate. Using crystal and glass beads instead of plastic keeps the colors clear and bright and adds a needed weight to the pieces. We used vibrant colors for our pieces that would be lively assets to your bridesmaids' outfits. These pieces also make a stunning gift for your mother or your future mother-in-law. For a lighter look, use clear and teal crystals together.

DIRECTIONS FOR RING

1. Thread 3 yards (2.7 m) of a single strand of bead string through the needle. Do not tie a knot at the end.

2. String six seed beads onto the thread, leaving about 2" (5.1 cm) of thread on the end (see fig. 1).

3. Form a circle of beads by pushing the needle and thread back through the first bead (see fig. 1).

4. String up one 4 mm crystal bead, followed by one 6 mm crystal bead, followed by another 4 mm crystal bead. These beads are labeled A, B, and C in fig. 2 .

5. Pull thread taut and wrap around the thread that runs in between seed beads five and six (see fig. 3). Pull needle back through crystal bead C. Pull taut. Crystal beads A and C will look perpendicular to seed bead circle. Bead B will be parallel to seed bead circle.

TIP *Bring a swatch of the bridesmaids' dress fabric to the bead store so you can coordinate the colors. You could also make these in shades of cream, white or whatever color you choose for your own wedding dress.*

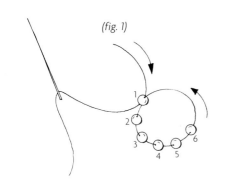

(fig. 1)

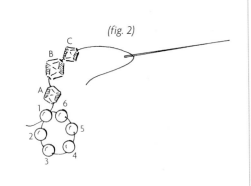

(fig. 2)

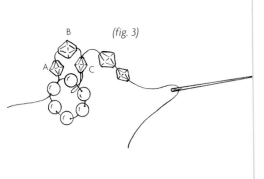

(fig. 3)

6. Add on another 6 mm crystal bead, followed by another 4 mm crystal bead and repeat the same process, this time wrapping needle and thread around existing thread in between seed beads five and four, then going back through the 4 mm crystal until you have formed the second petal.

7. Repeat this process until you have all six of the 6 mm crystals and all six of the 4 mm beads in place and have created the flower. Finish off flower by inserting the needle through the top of the first 4 mm bead.

8. Solidify the flower by running the needle and thread in a circle in through the holes of the 6 mm beads. Work your needle through the piece until it meets with the loose 2" (5.1 cm) end that you left hanging when you started your seed bead circle. Tie a square knot with your two end pieces. Weave the existing ends through the beads and then trim. The flower face should form a slight dome once the thread is pulled taut and tied off.

9. For the band, cut approximately 1 yard (.9 m) of the stretchable cord and single thread through eye of a bendable needle. Attach to flower by wrapping around thread in between two of the 6 mm beads on the outside edge of the flower. Leave 2" (5.1 cm) on the end for tying off later.

10. String on twenty-seven seed beads and insert needle on opposite side of flower (three 6 mm beads away), looping stretch thread around existing thread on flower in between two beads. Pull thread taut.

11. Place another twenty-seven seed beads onto the needle and bring the needle back through the original point where you began the band. Make a square knot with two ends of cord. Pull knot tight with needle-nose pliers and cut ends close. You could put a little dab of Super Glue onto the knot to secure it.

DIRECTIONS FOR NECKLACE

1. Make the center flower of the ring by following steps one through eight of the ring directions.

2. Add jump ring onto the piece by placing around the thread in between two beads. Close up with needle-nose pliers.

3. To make the ribbon necklace, cut a 20" (50.8 cm) length of ribbon, making sure to square up the edges of the ribbon as best as possible with the scissors. Thread 12" (30.5 cm) of

bead string onto the regular sewing needle. Knot the end of the bead string and run it through one end of the ribbon.

4. Run the ribbon and needle and thread through the hole in the bead tip, making sure to pull the entire end of the ribbon through the hole *(see fig. 4)*. Tie a few more knots at the end of the bead string to prevent the ribbon from slipping out of the bead tip. Cut the string and close up the bead tip with the needle-nose pliers.

5. Thread the free end of the ribbon through the flower pendant jump ring.

6. Repeat step four on the other end of the ribbon. Add a jump ring on one end of bead tip and clasp on other end. Close up jump ring with needle-nose pliers and your necklace is complete.

MATERIALS
FOR NECKLACE

24" (61 cm) of 3/8" (1 cm) colored silk organza or organdy ribbon

Two medium gold jump rings

One gold jewelry clasp

Two gold bead tips

One small package seed beads

Two bead tips

Six 4 mm crystal beads

Six 6 mm crystal beads

One package "no stretch" nylon bead string, size # 4 in coordinating color

Five bendable bead needles (small enough to fit through seed bead)

One regular sewing needle

Needle-nose pliers

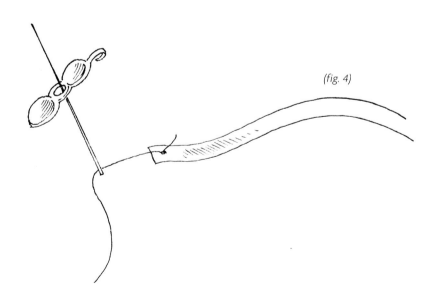

(fig. 4)

MATERIALS FOR BRACELET

Small seed beads

Small beads, just larger than seed beads, but large enough to accommodate three strands of wire through the hole

6 mm crystal beads

Fine beading wire

Two jump rings

Bracelet clasp

Needle-nose pliers

Scissors

DIRECTIONS FOR BRACELET

1. Cut three yard-long (meter-long) strands of beading wire. Twist the strands together on one end. Thread two medium beads onto the wires.

2. On the right and left strands, thread on nine seed beads. On the middle strand, thread one medium bead, one crystal, and another medium bead (*see fig. 5*).

VARIATION *This design also works great as a choker. Wrap a dressmaker's measuring tape around your neck to determine the length. Add a small length of chain to the end of the necklace to vary the size.*

3. Twist the three strands together twice, keeping the beads close together. Thread two medium beads onto the twisted strands. Separate the wires, and thread on beads as in step two *(see fig. 6)*.

4. Repeat the process until the bracelet measures a little longer than the size of the wearer's wrist. Both ends should be twisted, so the beading stays tight. Wrap each end around a jump ring and twist the wire back on itself to secure it. You can add a chain to one end for variable lengths.

5. Trim the excess. Attach the clasp pieces to the jump rings with needle-nose pliers.

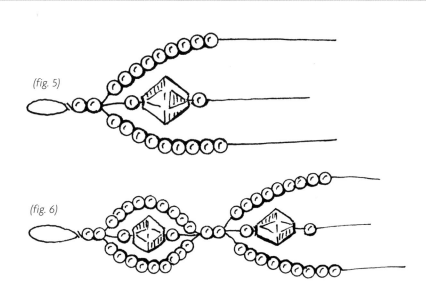

(fig. 5)

(fig. 6)

Mooning Over Memories

PAPER AND MOONSTONE FRAME

All too often the words "elegant" and "expensive" are used interchangeably. We know that you are horrified, too. Although some elegant items are amazingly expensive, the two are not inextricably linked—a mistake that is made over and over again, especially when weddings are concerned. We have faith that you can tell the difference. If you wonder if a designer hand-cut glass frame might go over better than this one, simply because it's costly, don't be too sure. (If you find yourself actually asking that question, it's time for an intervention.) People who like cut glass will prefer it, but the simplicity of this frame makes it striking.

Picture frames are a popular gift because they invite recipients to remember friends and family. However, they can be very expensive, especially when you are looking for something special. Instead of spending a bundle on frames that anyone can find, buy basic and transform it into a work of art itself. There won't be any others like it and the end result will have a prominent place in your friends' homes.

You can give the frame complete with a picture of the future bride and groom. Or, insert your favorite photo of you and the recipient.

VARIATION *You don't have to stick to small frames. Huge frames with small openings look stunning when combined with a subtly decorated paper. This technique works with any size frame as long as your paper is big enough. If you are having trouble finding paper big enough, consider wallpaper or wrapping paper.*

MATERIALS

One picture frame with flat surface and a 5" × 7" (12.7 cm × 17.8 cm) opening

One sheet 20" × 30" (50.8 cm × 76.2 cm) decorative paper

Roundstone sequins

Bone folder

Spray adhesive

Craft knife

Metal ruler

Sharp pencil

Craft glue

Cotton swab

1. Place sheet of decorative paper face down on cutting surface.

2. Remove glass and backing from picture frame and place frame face down, centering it on paper.

3. Draw a pencil line around outer edge of frame. Remove frame and place to the side.

4. Measure a rectangle that is one inch larger than the existing rectangle on all sides. Mark it with a pencil.

5. Cut out larger rectangle with a craft knife.

6. Place decorative paper face down on work surface and spray it with spray mount.

7. Center frame face down over paper.

8. Turn face up and burnish out any bubbles with your bone folder.

9. Turn face down and trim corners with craft knife as follows: Left and right edges can be cut square at 90° angles. Top and bottom edges should be cut at a 45° angle *(see fig. 1)*.

10. Fold in left and right edges of decorative paper to back of frame, scoring edges with bone folder and burnishing as you adhere them to the back of the frame.

11. Fold in top edges to back of frame in similar fashion.

(fig. 1)

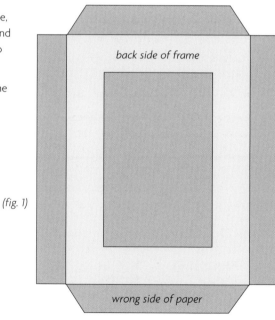

back side of frame

wrong side of paper

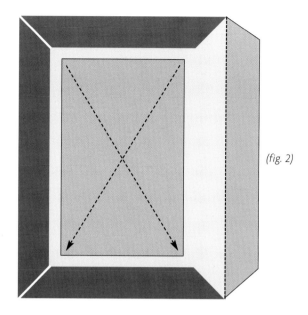

(fig. 2)

12. Cut an opening for the photo with a craft knife. Start in the upper left-hand corner and cut to the lower right-hand corner. Then cut from the upper right-hand corner to the lower left (see fig. 2).

13. Fold the paper flaps to the back side of the frame, scoring and burnishing the paper with your bone folder. Trim excess paper with craft knife.

14. Turn frame face up on the work surface. Finish off the inside corners by adding seven round-stones to each corner. Apply with cotton swab and a small dab of craft glue. Start with one at each corner and work your way out left and right until all seven have been placed. Use your craft knife to coax the moonstones into place.

15. Trim your favorite picture to fit. Clean the glass and put it back in the frame. Place photo and backing on frame.

TIP *You can use a paper that picks up some color, pattern, or feeling of the wedding itself. A lovely paper from your invitation will forever be echoed in the frame. Or, perhaps the dark olive tones of the restaurant's cashmere walls and teal beaded lights will resonate in a deep green paper and teal stones.*

Guest Survival Kit

HOTEL ROOM GOODIES

MATERIALS

**Mini lunch boxes,
one for each room**

Scissors

**Adhesive-backed
printer paper**

**Template from
page 294**

**Color photocopier
or scanner and
color printer**

CONTENTS
FOR THE KIT

**Maps, directions,
sewing kit, itinerary,
list of guests, travel
toothbrush, trail mix,
brownies, and so on**

When friends travel from out of town for a wedding, they immediately feel welcomed and excited about the festivities when they find these special packages waiting in their hotel rooms. A survival kit should include the basics for the weekend: maps (with locations highlighted), directions, and a schedule of events. Include some other useful items like a sewing kit, bottle opener, or travel toothbrush.

Add munchies for the late-night snack attacks as well as a special something from your favorite nearby bakery. Place the baked goods in a glassine or waxed paper envelope and seal with directions to the bakery so your friends can get their early morning java fix without feeling helpless. Complete the kit with a personal note and any amenities your friends might love, such as a great bath product, a sidecar bottle of wine, an eye mask, or a stuffed animal for the kids.

Talk to the hotel manager about the guest packages when you are arranging the reservations. On the morning of the arrival date, drop the packages at the hotel with name tags attached.

1. Print Guest Survival Kit logos on adhesive paper. Make color photocopies of the logo on page 294, or scan it into your computer and print copies in color. You can fit about eight on a page.

2. Cut out the Guest Survival Kit logos from the sticker paper.

3. Place the stickers on the lunch boxes.

4. Fill with contents, placing the munchies and note on top of the stack.

5. Tie a name tag on the handle and deliver the packages to the hotel.

VARIATION *If you can't find plain, inexpensive lunch boxes, check card stores for small, handled gift bags. Tie the handles together with the name tag and some curled ribbon.*

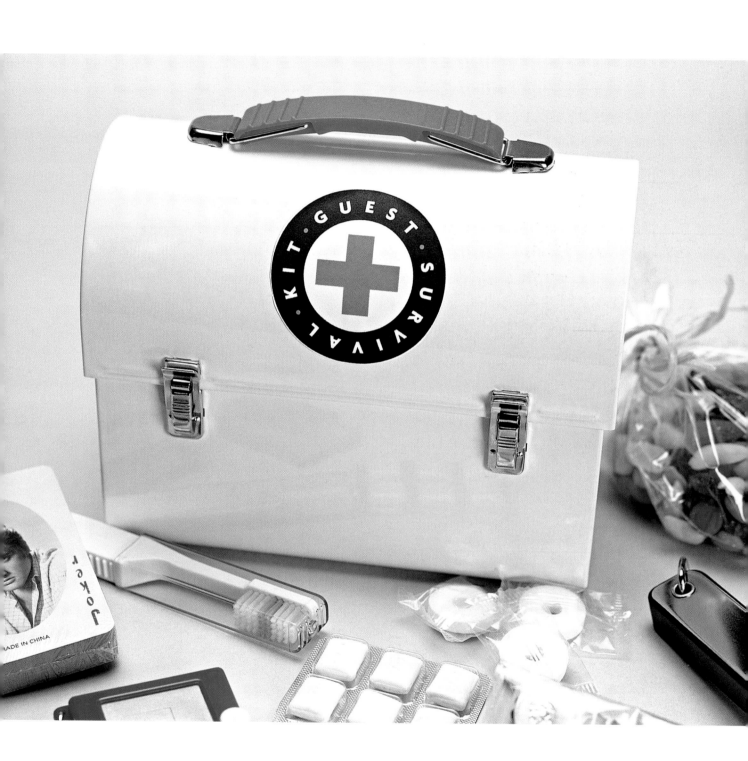

brian + pam

songs from our wedding 9.5.03

The Beat Goes On
MUSIC CD

Music is part of the scene. Whether it's Ella and Louis crooning during dinner or the best funk band in Pittsburgh blaring their horns across the crowded dance floor, music locks an event in memory. Send guests on their way with a melodic favor that will find a permanent home in their CD players.

Use your computer savvy to make a compilation of music, either from your wedding day or that you two have enjoyed together. Make a label and case insert and you have a swell-looking CD.

TO MAKE THE CD

1. Using a CD burner and the program installed on your computer, create a compilation and burn the CD. Allow yourself enough time to figure out the process, if you haven't done it before.

2. Listen to a few of the CDs to make sure there isn't a problem with the data transfer. Pop each CD into a jewel case and start on the inserts.

TO MAKE THE CD CASE INSERT AND LABEL

1. Using your favorite graphics program, create a horizontal document that is 9 $7/16$" x 4 $11/16$" (23.9 cm x 11.9 cm). The left half of the document will be the inside cover of your CD case. Choosing your favorite typeface and colors, write a list of the songs. You can also include a message from both of you to your guests—but you should keep it simple.

2. The right half of the document will be the cover of the CD case. Choose a favorite image, and give your CD a title. Print the inserts on photo-quality paper. Cut out the insert using a craft knife and a ruler or a paper trimmer. Fold the inserts in half and score with a bone folder. Slide the inserts into the inside covers of the CD jewel cases.

3. Arrange the cover photo and text to print on a CD label. Print a draft to line up everything. Print finished labels and stick on to burned CD.

TIP *Listen carefully to the words and sentiments of the songs you choose. There are plenty of great songs that are not emblematic of your wedding wishes. Even if you love "Boulevard of Broken Dreams," save it for a different CD. You don't have to be tame, but give some thought to the lyrics.*

MATERIALS

Personal computer

Color printer

CD burner

CD-R blank CDs (the kind you can burn in a computer or CD burner)

Plain CD jewel cases

Gloss white or silver foil adhesive CD labels that work with your model color printer

Photo-quality paper, 8 $1/2$" × 11" (21.6 cm × 27.9 cm)

Craft knife or paper trimmer

Ruler

Bone folder

Cuppa Quiet
PAINT-YOUR-OWN-POTTERY TEA KIT

MATERIALS

An idea for a design, simpler is better

A selection of teas and tea accessories to fit inside the cup

Interesting paper

Decorative-edge scissors

Small hole punch

String

Sometimes a quiet evening with a hot cup of tea is just the relaxation we need when life gets busy. That goes for both you and your friends. Give your shower guests or bridal party a lead on an evening curled up with a hot cuppa and a book. Start at a paint-your-own-pottery store and pick out the biggest latte cups they have. Take along a Walkman and enjoy the time to yourself (with your busy life, you know how rare that is already). You can personalize them for each guest. After a few days, your creations will be ready to pick up. Fill them with your favorite selection of teas. Add some crystal sugar and a book to round out the gift.

1. Sketch out your design on the cup and saucer with a regular No. 2 pencil. The marks from this pencil will burn off in the firing process. If you want a mark that will show after firing, ask for an underglaze pencil.

2. Paint your design with the underglaze paints. You will need three to four coats for a vibrant finished project, or one to two coats for a watercolor look. Many stores have squeeze bottles of paints for writing, so you can add names, dates, and messages to your design. Leave the cups and saucers to be fired. They should be ready in a few days.

3. Fill the cup with teas and accessories. Choose either favorites or something straightforward and simple, like an English Breakfast or Earl Grey. For a special treat, try the amazing teas from Mariage Frères in Paris. You can order them by mail (see Resources).

4. Cut a 1" x 1" (2.5 cm x 2.5 cm) square of paper with the decorative-edge scissors. Punch a small hole in the tag and thread a string through it, anchored with a knot. Write a message on the tag and tape the end of the string inside the cup, lopping the tag over the rim.

SHORTCUT *Don't fret if you don't have a lot of time. You can buy nicely decorated latte cups, too. Just apply your creativity to the label and contents.*

Knickers with a Twist

PERSONALIZED PANTIES FOR YOUR PALS

MATERIALS FOR SCOUT PATCH

"Scout green" underwear

Girl Scout or Boy Scout patches

Matching thread

Needle

Scissors

Straight pins

Beautiful articles with age-old refinement make terrific gifts. But for your closest friends, familiarity and humor count the most. Forget the garish lingerie that often circulates at these occasions and opt for a wittier approach. These undies may be a little daring, but they are going to your nearest gal pals…who will most certainly get a laugh. All you need is a little inventiveness and a willingness to exploit some pure and wholesome materials.

Personalize your pit crew's (a.k.a bridesmaids') undies with a homemade gas station attendant's patch. Simply handwrite each of the bridesmaid's names on the patches and do a basic backstitch in embroidery thread. Or sew on a bowling patch and your girlfriends will have a spare to go with their Campers and bowling shirts. You can even give out some merit badges to the gals that deserve them the most (your scout troop was always prepared, you know). If patches are not readily available in your area, log onto to eBay.com, look under patches, and play to win. This project works great with boxers, too!

DIRECTIONS FOR SCOUT PATCH

1. Align patches on front of underwear and pin in place.

2. Sew patches on underwear.

3. Trim threads with scissors.

TIP *Complete the gift by packaging the undies in containers that go with the theme. The scout panties can be wrapped in a bandana, the gas station attendant's in a funnel, and the bowling undies in a bowling bag.*

MATERIALS FOR
BOWLING PATCH

Black underwear

Bowling patch

Matching thread

Needle

Scissors

Straight pins

Red embroidery
thread

Embroidery needle

Tracing paper

Pencil

DIRECTIONS FOR BOWLING PATCH

1. Align patch on front of underwear and pin in place.

2. Sew patch on underwear.

3. Trim threads with scissors.

4. Handwrite attendant's name in cursive on tracing paper in pencil. Center paper under bowling ball patch and pin into place.

5. Thread about 3 yards (2.7 m) of single-thread embroidery floss through the embroidery needle. Pull the needle up through the beginning of your letter form, leaving about 1" (2.5 cm) of loose thread. Do not tie off.

6. Embroider the name through the layer of tracing paper. Do a simple backstitch until you've completed embroidering the name. Do not tie off the end. Weave the thread back through your piece to secure ends. Trim both ends of loose thread.

7. Pull off tracing paper layer.

DIRECTIONS FOR GAS STATION ATTENDANT PATCH

1. Copy oval template from page 294. Center over twill iron-on patch. Pin in place and cut out shape. Place a piece of tracing paper over the patch and trace the outline of the shape. Handwrite attendant's name in cursive on the tracing paper oval in pencil, centering the name in the oval as best you can.

2. Pin the oval tracing paper to the oval twill patch.

3. Thread about 3 yards (2.7 m) of single-thread embroidery floss through the embroidery needle. Pull needle up through the beginning of your letter form, leaving about 1" (2.5 cm) of loose thread. Do not tie off.

4. Embroider the name through the layer of tracing paper. Do a simple backstitch until you've completed embroidering the name. Do not tie off the end. Weave the thread back through your piece to secure ends. Trim both ends of loose thread.

5. Pull off tracing paper layer.

6. Preheat iron for 8 minutes. Do not add water. Iron underwear flat.

7. Position patch on underwear front and iron onto panty. Make sure you do not iron the elastic waistband because it will melt.

8. Measure out a 12" (30.5 cm) length of the soutache braid and place along outer edge of patch.

9. Take braid off patch and place to the side. Run a thin line of fabric glue along outer edge of patch. Starting at center bottom, place braid around edge and glue into place. The ends may fray a little, so put an extra dab of glue at the ends to stop this from happening. Overlap the ends a tiny bit and trim to fit. Let glue set about 20 minutes.

10. Topstitch soutache braid in place either by hand or with a machine.

VARIATION *Customize the patches to your friends' personalities and tastes. Most sewing and army and navy stores offer a wide array of patches with which you can coordinate the panty colors.*

MATERIALS FOR GAS STATION ATTENDANT PATCH

Dark blue cotton underwear

White or off-white twill iron-on patches

Oval template from page 294

Tracing paper

Pencil

³/₃₂" (2.4 mm) red no-iron soutache braid

Red embroidery thread

Embroidery needle

Fabric glue

Red sewing thread

Sewing needle

Scissors

Straight pins

4" × 6" × ³/₄"
(10.2 cm × 15.2 cm × 1.9
cm) cardboard gift box

4" × 6"
(10.2 cm × 15.2 cm)
sheet of ¹/₁₆" thick
(1.6 cm) Plexiglas

Spray adhesive

Craft knife

Red book cloth

Drafting triangle

Metal ruler

Pencil

Template
from page 294

Color photocopier or
scanner and printer

8 ¹/₂" × 11"
(21.6 cm × 27.9 cm)
glossy photo paper

Awl

Three 4 mm
ball bearings

Black fine-tip
permanent marker

Bone folder

Small container of
adhesive solvent,
such as Bestine

Cotton swab

Maybe, Baby!

RETRO BALL BEARING TOY

Most guests will recognize the familiar sound of this toy, the soft sound of steel balls rolling on paperboard in search of the high score. Combine that with a groan of exasperation followed by a whoop of success, and you complete the memory. The retro design of this favor is perfect for this age-old occasion and gives people a little something to fidget with during conversations or a break in dancing. Instead of a maze or rockets heading to space, this toy features a comic book–style matrimony moment. If, however, you prefer rockets heading to space….

1. Color photocopy the illustration from page 294 onto high-quality paper stock. Or scan it and print it on your color printer, on glossy photo paper. Trim edges with craft knife and ruler.

2. Pierce a hole in each of the "Yes," "No," and "Maybe" circles with an awl. Color in any rough edges with the black marker.

3. Spray mount back of the illustration and paste it into the box. Drop in the three ball bearings.

4. Measure, then cut out a piece of 6" x 8" (15.2 cm x 20.3 cm) book cloth, using pencil, triangle, ruler, and craft knife.

5. Lay fabric wrong side up. Place box in dead center of material and trace the outside of the box onto the fabric with a pencil.

VARIATION *You may want to make up your own graphic, use a photo, or find a postcard. Use your imagination to customize the game to your own taste.*

(fig. 1)

fold flap in

(fig. 2)

6. Spray mount the wrong side of the material. Return box to dead center and burnish it in place with the bone folder. Then turn right-side up and place the Plexiglas on top of box.

7. Cut fabric corners on the short sides at 90° angles and long sides at 45° angles *(see fig. 1)*.

8. Fold and burnish material onto long sides of box with your bone folder. Fold and burnish material onto short sides of box. *(see fig. 2)*.

9. Continue folding and burnishing onto the Plexiglas top of the box. Trim corners at a 45° angle.

10. Trim border on top to about ⅛" (3 mm) with craft knife and metal ruler.

11. Clean off excess adhesive with Bestine and a cotton swab.

Adapting Style

No doubt about it. You've got style. The great thing about your style is that it gives you a trademark to stamp on everything. A wedding is the best time to let your style be your guide. Of course, we're in favor of letting your style guide you all the time, from the pen you use to the eyeglasses you wear. At a wedding, you host a gathering for a special reason, and every bit of it should let guests know that it is your wedding. That is, yours and your fiancé's. What good is a wedding—a union—if it only reflects the style of one of you? Not very stylish at all, we think.

CHANGING PROJECTS TO FIT

Adapting a project to fit your style isn't very hard at all. At first it may feel difficult, because projects list materials and colors...and (you might think) pretty much dictate a style. But the materials lists are meant to be changed. The projects are inspiration waiting for your direction, to adapt them to fit your needs and your style. Change the papers used to those that you think are beautiful, or those that go with the season. Change any element to make it more your own.

If a project is too floral for you, you don't have to eliminate the project from your repertoire—change the flowers into dots, clouds, or whatever is up your alley. If you already have an invitation ordered from your favorite stationers, look at invitation projects in a different light, instead of skipping over them. The same concept can be adapted to make a mini photo album cover, a menu, a welcome card to place in a hotel room, or a program. Let your brain play with projects and develop ways to to fit your needs. These projects can be taken apart and re-created as your own.

BALANCING STYLES

It takes a little work to identify your particular style— especially if it is eclectic. You might like woodsy items and lace, as well as pop items that add humor and modern style. The key to making it all work is to find a balance.

If you like flowers, you *could* make everything floral— but that would be overkill. The flowers might invade everything and lose their significance or beauty. Balance the textures and bright colors of flowers with smooth lines and sleek colors. A smooth silver iZone guest book (see page 284) used in a flower-heavy wedding will stand out as an elegant and fun item. At the same time it will give the flowers a greater effect on the setting.

Likewise, if you opt for all pop and kitsch, your wedding and reception could feel cold and even sarcastic. Warm it up by adding a touch of the opposite style: Add a small cut flower to each place assignment chair (see page 288) or use a woodsy paper on the card box (see page 276). Subtly blending in other textures balances the effect. Lines are softened, heavy textures are tempered with elegance and sleek additions. Guests will feel at ease because your style is balanced. ✳

Ceremony Details

A wedding ceremony is a personal moment you share with those closest to you—unless you've invited 1,000 people. More importantly, it's a time you share with the one person closest to you, and the ceremony details should fit both of you. Not surprisingly, many ceremony details are dictated by the officiating body. Depending on where you've chosen to get married, and by whom, you may have to adhere to certain guidelines. Some places may insist that you leave a pause for anyone to object (despite *your* objection to the idea), others may not let your best-friend-opera-star sing a note. But you can always find those that will even let you have a juggler if you so desire (why not?). We feel pretty confident that you'll check out the entire ceremony to make sure you get what you want. After all, there's no sense in paying attention to the details if you don't look at the overall experience as well. The result of your efforts will be a meaningful ceremony that highlights the essence of your personalities and your shared history.

But once the mechanics of the ceremony are addressed, how can you personalize the look? We assembled some details that will add your own style to the standard elements. When you pick out your dress, the flowers, and the menswear, the easiest element for a unique twist is you. For that reason, we've designed some jewelry, headwear, and shoes for you to adapt to your colors or style. We've also included a pillow the ring bearer will be glad to hold.

MATERIALS

¹⁄₄ (22.9 cm) yard
cotton poplin

Scissors

1 yard (.9 m) of 4 ¹⁄₂"
(11.4 cm) wide light
blue organdy
or organza ribbon

1 yard (.9 m) of 4 ¹⁄₂"
(11.4 cm) wide
white organdy or
organza ribbon

1 yard (.9 m) of ¹⁄₄"
(6.4 mm) wide
light blue organdy
or organza ribbon

Straight pins

Small bag cotton
pillow stuffing

Silver seed beads

Tin letters
"L, O, V, E"

White
sewing thread

Needle

Sewing machine

Drafting triangle

Ruler

Sewing pencil
or marker

Cushion of Love

RING BEARER'S PILLOW

What can one say about the function of a ring bearer's pillow? Usually not much beyond its status as the highly guarded accessory of one young wedding participant. What makes this pillow so special? The punched tin letters juxtaposed against the fragile-looking organza and sparkly seed beads adds an unexpected industrial edge to a delicate, soft object. You can read into the combination of opposites all you like, we won't object. But the overall effect is that the word "LOVE" pops out very well because it is a sharper, cooler material than the background.

1. Measure and cut an 8" (20.3 cm) square of cotton poplin.

2. Measure and cut two 8" (20.3 cm) strips of the 4½" (11.4 cm) wide white ribbon and two 8" (20.3 cm) strips of the blue ribbon.

3. Basket weave the four strips together. Lay one white ribbon vertically on the work surface. Lay one blue ribbon horizontally over the white ribbon. Lay the second white ribbon vertically to the left of the first white ribbon. Lay the second blue ribbon parallel to the other blue ribbon. Flip up the end of the first white ribbon and lay it over the second blue ribbon. The ribbons will form what looks like four quadrants. Pin these together with straight pins.

VARIATION *For a more personalized approach, substitute the word "LOVE" with the bride and groom's first and last initials.*

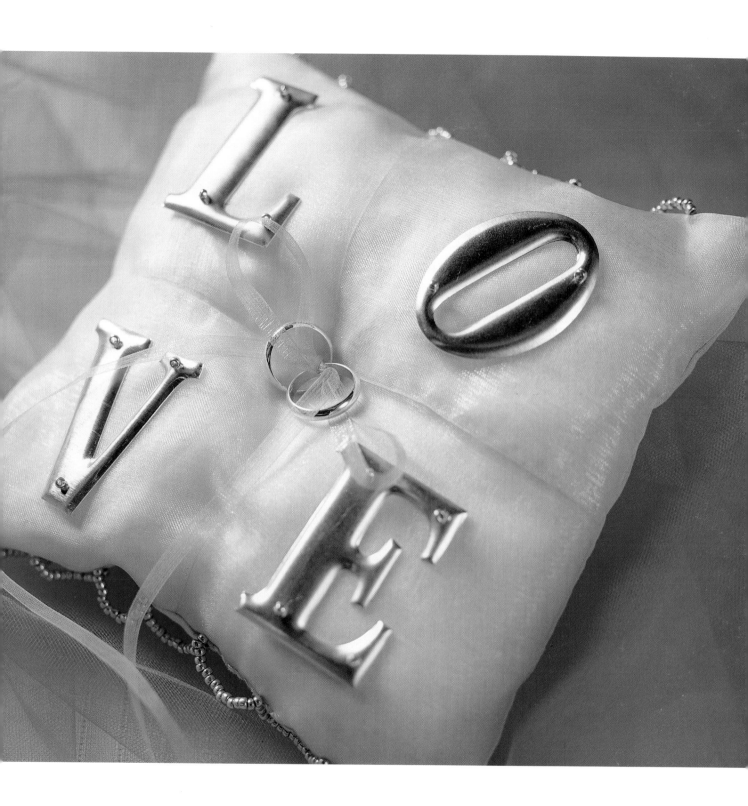

4. Topstitch the ribbons onto a cotton square, leaving about $^3/_8$" (1 cm) all around.

5. Center, then hand sew the letters "L, O, V, and E" to each of the quadrants of the ribbon so it matches the photograph: Start sewing through the bottom of the ribbon, then through the letter hole. Thread a seed bead onto the needle. Go back through the letter hole again and knot and cut the ends. Continue this process until all the letters have been sewn onto the ribbon.

6. Place letter side of fabric face down over other cotton square. Pin two sides together.

7. Sew a $^1/_2$" (1.3 cm) seam all around, leaving a $3 ^1/_2$" (8.9 cm) seam opening along the bottom edge to turn the piece right-side out. Trim the corners of the newly sewn seam to reduce fabric bulk. Turn the pillow right-side out.

8. Stuff the pillow and blind stitch the seam opening.

TIP *You can use either gold or silver seed beads to accent the piece. Gold seed beads would coordinate best with gold rings, silver seed beads with platinum rings.*

9. Make tick marks every $3/4$" (1.9 cm) on top and bottom edges of pillow. Thread 2 yards (1.8 m) of a double strand of thread on the needle. Insert needle into pillow's lower left corner and knot the loose end. String up fifteen seed beads, then sew back into pillow at first tick mark *(see fig. 1)* Continue doing this, creating a scalloped pattern until you've reached the lower right corner of the pillow. Do the same on top of the pillow. Knot and trim ends.

10. Sew the center point of the $1/4$" (6.4 mm) wide blue ribbon into the center of the pillow. Pass the needle and thread through all of the layers of batting and fabric. Leave the loose end on top of the pillow without tying the loose end. On the back side of the pillow, thread a seed bead through the needle. Then pass the needle back through all the layers of the pillow. Sew through the center point of the $1/4$" (6.4 mm) ribbon, through a seed bead and back through the ribbon. Tie both thread loose ends together on the underside of the ribbon. Make sure the ribbon feels very secure, as it will be holding your rings.

11. Thread your rings onto the ribbon and tie it in a bow.

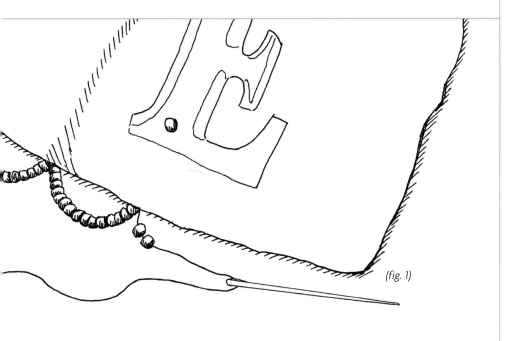

(fig. 1)

Practical Princess-Wear

SUBTLE TIARA

Everyone should have a tiara to wear to state dinners, shopping, and baseball games. For your wedding, it should be a very nice one. Put Harry Winston's on hold (not that any of us want to, mind you), and craft your own that will look sensible and delicate without the need for an armed escort. The materials and method are incredibly simple, but the finished product won't show that at all.

1. Use the measuring tape to find the center point of your headband.

2. Pull out about 3 yards (2.7 m) of wire. Wrap the center of the wire once around the center of the band (see fig. 1).

3. String on five seed beads (this may vary according to the width of your band). Wrap around width of headband and to the right of the center point. Pull tightly. The five seed beads should cover the width of the headband. You may need more or fewer beads for each wraparound.

4. Wrap wire around headband tightly again, this time without adding on the five seed beads. This will secure the beads.

5. Continue steps three and four (see figs. 2-3), wrapping wire and adding beads until you have fifty rows of seed beads. Make sure bead rows rest snuggly against each other, without wire showing through. Secure wire on end by wrapping it back through the piece in between the bead rows three or four times. Cut end and tuck in between bead rows using your fingernail to wedge it into place.

6. Starting back at the center point, repeat steps two through five, this time working the other side of the center point.

TIP *If you want to wear a veil with the tiara, sew the veil onto both ends of your beadwork.*

MATERIALS

One spool heavy-guage craft wire

One white or cream cloth-covered headband with boning inside

One container white seed beads

Twenty 4 mm silver and clear crystals

Ten 6 mm clear crystals

Sewing measuring tape

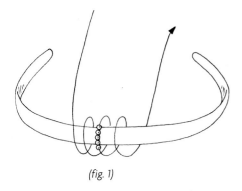

(fig. 1)

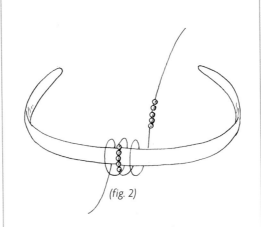

(fig. 2)

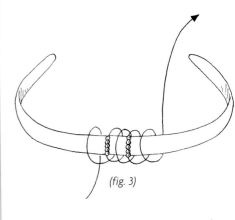

(fig. 3)

7. You are now ready to top the tiara. Starting on the left-hand side of the piece, wrap the wire around the headband once or twice, securing it between bead rows.

8. Add on six white seed beads followed by one 4 mm crystal, followed by one 6 mm crystal, followed by another 4 mm crystal, followed by six more seed beads *(see fig. 4)*.

9. Count in ten rows from the end of the headband and wrap the wire around the headband between rows ten and eleven *(see fig. 5)*.

10. Add on six more white seed beads followed by one 4 mm crystal, followed by one 6 mm crystal, followed by another 4 mm crystal, followed by six more seed beads. Wrap wire around between rows twenty and twenty-one.

11. Repeat this process, wrapping around every tenth row until you and make it to row one hundred.

12. Secure wire on end by wrapping it back through the piece between the bead rows three or four times. Cut end and tuck in between bead rows using your fingernail to wedge it into place.

VARIATION *Use colored beads to match the color of your dress. Ivory-colored seed beads with clear peach crystals are a great combination for an ivory-colored dress.*

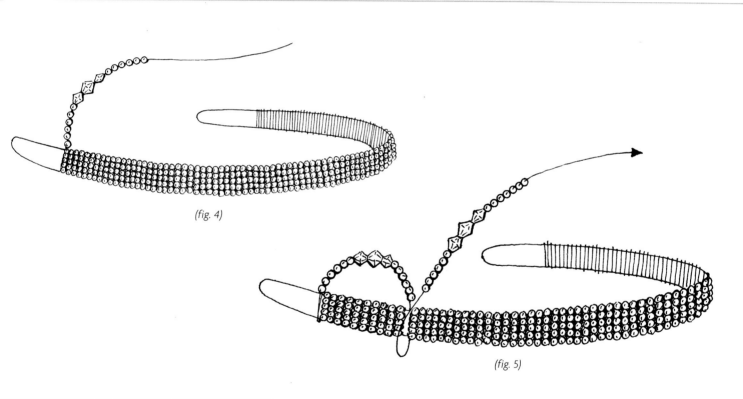

(fig. 4)

(fig. 5)

Twinkle Toes

SHOE DECORATIONS

**MATERIALS FOR
BEADED SHOE**

**One pair of
wedding sandals**

**Four cream or
white silk leaves with
wire stems**

**28-gauge
beading wire**

**Ten pink
freshwater pearls**

**Small container
of silver seed beads**

**Small container of
white seed beads**

**Small container of
clear seed beads**

Scissors

Flowers are lively accents—especially when peeking out from beneath the hem of a long dress. Even though your feet may feel like wilting after the long evening you have planned, real flowers would fall flat much sooner than that. Silk flowers will survive the scuffle of a march down the aisle and multiple turns on the dance floor.

DIRECTIONS FOR BEADED SHOE

1. Pull out about 2 yards (1.8 m) of beading wire and cut.

2. String five freshwater pearls and form a circle, leaving 2" (5.1 cm) of loose wire on the end.

3. Overlap short end of wire and pull the circle tight *(see fig. 1)*.

4. Add five silver seed beads to the long end of wire *(see fig. 2)*.

5. Wrap wire around other side of freshwater pearl, in between pearls one and two and pull wire tight.

6. Add five more silver beads and repeat the process, this time wrapping wire around between beads two and three *(see fig. 3)*.

7. Add five more silver beads and repeat the process again, going in between beads three and four, and so on until you've completed the circle. Wrap wire around and tighten between beads one and five.

8. String an assortment of clear and white seed beads until you have strung up eleven beads onto the bead wire.

9. Wrap the wire around between beads one and two and pull wire tight. Repeat this process again and again until you have completed a full circle *(see fig. 4)*.

TIP *Look for a shoe that has a somewhat narrow, simple band on the front. It will be easier to wrap the wire around and will show off the shoe decoration better.*

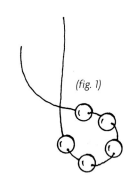

(fig. 1)

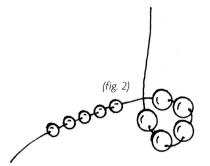

(fig. 2)

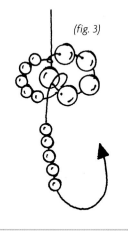

(fig. 3)

10. Weave long end of wire back through the piece to reinforce and stabilize the beaded flower.

11. Join wire ends together and tie off. Do not cut long end of wire.

12. Wire on one freshwater pearl to the center of the flower and weave through piece on underside to secure.

13. Cut silk leaves to desired size. Place horizontally on sandal front making a mirror image of the leaves on either side, leaves facing out, stems facing in. Wrap stems around midpoint of sandal front.

14. Add flower to center front of sandal and wrap around sandal with remaining wire from step eleven. When flower is secure, wrap a little remaining wire under the flower and trim wire end.

15. Repeat on second shoe and get ready to strut down that aisle.

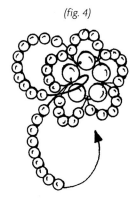

(fig. 4)

**MATERIALS
FOR SILK FLOWER
FOOTWEAR**

**One pair of
wedding sandals**

**Two white silk flowers,
no larger than 3" (7.6 cm)
when flattened**

**Two daisy party
favor flowers**

**Two green silk leaves
with wire stems**

28-gauge beading wire

Scissors

DIRECTIONS FOR SILK FLOWER FOOTWEAR

1. Remove stems, pistils, and stamens from flowers, leaving just the petals.

2. Insert daisy into center of flower and wrap remaining daisy wire around front part of sandal.

3. Cut silk leaves down to desired size and twist stems under flower base.

4. Use additional beading wire to further reinforce flower and leaves onto shoe.

5. Repeat process on second shoe.

Dynamic Collar
METAL AND BEAD CHOKER

This stunning wire-and-bead choker necklace assures a one-of-a-kind ensemble. Of course, every bride wants to look unique. Although you'll look divine in a simple pearl necklace, some outfits cry out for a gutsier approach—and we're all for that.

We used silver wire for our necklace, but choose the metal color that matches your jewelry (gold if your rings are gold, silver if they are platinum), and have fun with the making. Try it on at your dress fitting to make sure the necklines go well together. If you can't get past the idea of doing without pearls, but you long for jewelry that is more exciting than a strand, brava! Just use freshwater pearl beads like we did here, available at finer bead supply stores.

MATERIALS

One spool 26-gauge silver beading wire

One small container silver seed beads

Thirteen 6 mm light pink freshwater pearls

Seventy-two 4 mm clear crystal beads

One three-holed silver clasp

Heavy-duty scissors for cutting wire

1. Measure out and cut three strands of silver beading wire approximately 1 ½ yards (1.4 m) each.

2. Loop and twist about 3" (7.6 cm) of the wire on the end (*see fig. 1*).

3. Add six silver seed beads onto the left wire. Add six silver seed beads onto the right wire. String one pearl onto the center wire.

4. Gather beads as tightly as you can, twisting the wire tightly four times to hold the beads in place (*see fig. 2*).

5. Add a 4 mm crystal onto the right wire leaving about ¼" (6.4 mm) of slack on your wire (*see fig. 3*).

6. Fold the wire back to last twisted area (*see A in fig. 4*) and begin twisting wire again tightly for four rotations (*see fig. 5*).

TIP *It's a good idea to do a little practice run with this project to get the twisting technique consistent. Don't worry if some of your twists are a little longer or shorter. This will add to the charm of the piece.*

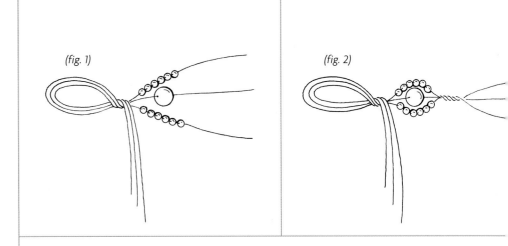

(fig. 1)

(fig. 2)

7. Add another 4 mm crystal onto the same wire. Repeat steps five and six two times until you have three 4 mm beads secured on the right wire.

8. Follow steps five to seven on the left wire until the arrangement of crystal beads looks like *fig. 6* with three beads on the right and left wires, no beads on the center wire.

9. Gather wires together at the bases of the twisted sections. Twist all three wires together tightly four rotations. Arrange the six wires with bead attachments until this section of the necklace forms a star *(see detail photo on facing page)*.

10. Repeat steps one through nine until you have thirteen sets of pearl beads framed by the silver seed beads and twelve sets of the star arrangement.

11. To finish off the piece, untwist beginning loop from step two. Twist wire ends of choker four times on each end. Add three silver seed beads to each of the wires and pull each wire through a hole on the clasp. (If the necklace fits a little large or small, add or subtract beads here for a proper fit.) Feed each loose wire end back through three seed beads and trim with heavy-duty scissors.

TIP *Choose beads that reflect the colors of your wedding material, whether that be bridesmaids' dresses, fiancé's accoutrements, or boutonniere.*

(fig. 3)

1/4"

(fig. 4)

A

(fig. 5)

(fig. 6)

Guided by Ancestors

Tradition is a funny thing. Some of us go out of our way to be free from it. Others are warmed by the prospect of continuing actions that originated generations before we were born. It links us to the past and to others who follow the same traditions.

How does that relate to weddings? Almost inextricably. In your everyday life, you are able to choose which traditions to perpetuate, stop, or initiate. However, it can be very difficult to remove a traditional element from a wedding. Why? Many people don't want to do anything that could sever their ties from peers or family, even if they don't like an element of the tradition. Oddly enough, it can be much easier to let our great grandparents make a decision about our wedding day than it is to make a decision of our own. With the stress that the weight of tradition brings, it's no wonder.

Tradition is precarious because it can be both helpful and restrictive. It forms a structure for you to wrap your experience around, which can help you immensely as you try to form a meaningful and memorable event. Tradition lets guests know what is coming and it lets you know what others expect of you. But it can also feel suffocating. If you like some traditional elements, but find others distasteful, it can be difficult to follow the ones you like and dispense with the others. How can you follow one tradition and reject another? The answer is simple: You just do. If you don't want to wear a white dress, then don't. Don't let history make that decision for you. Queen Victoria wore a white dress because she thought it was beautiful, not because everyone else wore one. Make your own choices.

Pay close attention to your thoughts as you contemplate changing, removing, or even elaborating traditions. Take care that you make every decision on purpose. Make sure every element of your wedding is what you want and what makes sense to you—not just what everyone in town does. That goes for all elements, traditional or not. If you want a three-tiered wedding cake just like everyone in your family has done for decades, make that decision because that is the cake you want, not because it is the one your family expects.

COMPROMISES

Every now and then (okay, every day) an iconoclast marries someone who values traditions. Learning how to communicate what you want, and learning to accept what someone else requires is nothing new to you. This is the perfect time to put that skill into full swing. If you're not the traditional type, you may have to learn to appreciate some traditions anyway. We know you'll be great at it.

THE CRAFT CONNECTION

What does tradition have to do with crafts? Plenty. Tradition affects the style of your wedding, what you do at the reception, and any number of things leading up to the wedding. Some of these controlling traditions may be cultural, others are familial. If every reception in the family has been a sit-down dinner, you probably feel comfortable following the same format. Crafts let you add your own stamp with unique centerpieces and a guest book that set your nuptials apart from anyone else's, regardless of the common features. Tradition is not a cookie-cutter, after all. It is an inspiration and a starting point. Use that inspiration to include meaningful elements that invoke your humor, wit, and style. ✳

Reception & Décor

A wedding is, essentially, a celebration with an official ceremony. The reception is a chance for your friends and family to celebrate your happiness and joy. It is also your opportunity to thank them for their love and support. Throw them a good party.

No matter what size the reception is, you know to cover the basics.

* Never leave your guests for long periods of time. Keep the photo sessions to a tight schedule and hustle the bustle. At one wedding we attended, we calculated that the bride and groom had only 4 minutes to spend with each guest! Don't waste time away from the people you've invited.

* Give people the right amount of food for the time of day. Serve food that you love to eat.

* Provide some entertainment in the form of music, dancing, or dining.

* Explain things. Many people choose their wedding activities from the same giant menu of traditions. If you are writing your own menu (bravo!), you may need to explain some elements that may be unfamiliar, either in a program or by announcement. Guests will feel most comfortable and ready to celebrate when they know what's going on.

A reception is more than a post-ceremony get-together. It is an experience, and you are in charge of the ambiance. Know which elements are important to you and which you want to let go. We believe you should pay some attention to the details and objects that people see, but the guests are the real focus. We feel pretty sure that the people you know are cool enough to take to the dance floor or make conversation, regardless of the details. What you want to do is encourage that natural liveliness and match the reception details to your personalities—so up the charm.

The reception should be comfortable and should contribute to your guests' experiences. This chapter is filled with ideas to enhance the party-half of the day. From centerpieces to favors, and card boxes to guest books, these projects give you ways to personalize your reception and live it up! Think through the event and imagine what people might want, how they might feel, and what they might need. If you approach it from their point of view and think about their enjoyment (as well as your own), you can't go wrong. What better way to celebrate the special day than by being perfect hosts together?

Hunka Burnin' Love

PHOTO VOTIVE

MATERIALS

Off-white pillar candle,
about 6" (15.2 cm) high

Four to seven
photo strips of you
and your partner
taken at a
photo booth

8½" × 11"
(21.6 cm × 27.9 cm)
vellum

White inkjet
or laser paper

Photocopier or
printer and scanner

Glue stick

A great evening like this calls for some pretty special lighting. The soft, warm light of candles takes the edge off restaurant or ballroom lighting and creates intimate gatherings at each table. The glow of lightly fluttering flames softens surroundings and, let's face it, everyone looks great in a little candlelight. Rather than opt for plain candles, use pictures to make mini beacons of love. Since many guests may not have seen you and your sweetie in a while, these votives can help them feel as if they have been closer than geography may allow. When the wick is lit, the emanating light illuminates the vellum images wrapped around the candle.

1. Copy photo strips onto vellum. Either take the photos to a local copy center or scan them with your computer and print them on special inkjet- or laser-compatible vellum. Both color and black-and-white copies work well. Line up several of the photo strips across the copier or scanner bed. Butt the strips against each other so they are tight and parallel. The long edge of the photo strips should run across the short dimension of the paper.

2. Reduce the size of the photos so that the strip is the height of the candle: in the featured candle, 6" (15.2 cm). You will have to print two copies in order to cover the circumference of your candle, 11" (27.9 cm). Mesh the two pieces by overlapping by ⅛" (3 mm) of the nonprinted edges. (You might want to print up a trial run on regular paper.)

3. Wrap the paper around the candle pillar and trim so there is no more than ¼" (6.4 mm) overlap.

4. Glue seams with a glue stick.

5. Place on a bed of uncooked rice in the center of each table.

VARIATION *Looking for a unique unity candle? Make a larger, taller version of this votive and use it during the ceremony. Simply use a 12" (30.5 cm) pillar candle. Enlarge the photos and print on a larger piece of vellum. Measure the circumference of the candle with a string to help you size the photos.*

The Ties That Bind

JAPANESE-STYLE PHOTO ALBUM

These Japanese-style photo albums are elegant and popular. There's a reason for that: they're lovely. They're also *très cher* in our favorite boutiques, where you'll soon see that the beauty translates rather swiftly into price, with numbers easily in excess of $90. Although this project is not easy, it is doable—and you can choose all the materials to fit your tastes instead of searching for a ready-made album to match your size requirements or style.

With projects that test the mettle of your craft skills, it is especially important to start well before the big day. In fact, it is important to finish it well before the wedding. Just set aside time to get it done (see "Budgeting Time" on page 28) and be realistic. Although we firmly believe that you must give yourself some leeway when it comes to schedules, you certainly don't want to return from your honeymoon with photos in hand and a half-assembled album to house them. Many wedding photos have languished in boxes in basements around the world for want of the perfect place to display them. (You wondered what was in those boxes, didn't you?) Should you leave the more complex projects to other people? Absolutely not! Items that you make for other people mean a lot because they are made by your own hands. Don't discount yourself—give yourself the best you can.

VARIATION *You can make these albums any size. To make the larger album in photo, we changed the dimensions to 16 1/4" x 13" (41.3 cm x 33 cm) and we didn't include the window. Simply make the height of the spine equal to the height of the cover board.*

MATERIALS FOR SMALLER ALBUM WITH WINDOW

Two sheets 13" × 20" (33 cm × 51 cm) book board

Two sheets of cream-colored 30" × 40" (76.2 cm × 101.6 cm) watercolor paper

Two sheets 20" × 30" (51 cm × 76.2 cm) decorative paper (hand block printed or wallpaper)

One sheet of book cloth

Utility knife

Craft knife

Bone folder

Manual or motorized drill

One 9/32" (7.1 mm) drill bit

C-clamps

One jar PVA glue

One bookbinder's brush

Metal ruler

Sharp pencil

Drafting triangle

3 yards (2.7 m) of 1/2" or 3/4" (1.3 cm or 1.9 cm) wide organdy or organza ribbon

Photo corners

Embroidery needle

Embroidery thread

Large newsprint tablet

White eraser

25" × 30" (63.5 cm × 76.2 cm) wooden board

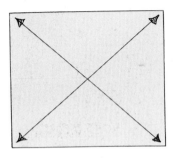

(fig. 1)

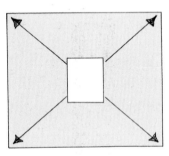

(fig. 2)

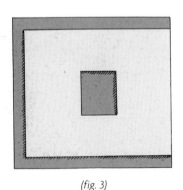

(fig. 3)

DIRECTIONS FOR SMALLER ALBUM

1. Measure two boards 12" wide x 10 ½" high (30.5 cm x 26.7 cm) with pencil and ruler. Use your triangle to square everything up, holding it against top and bottom edges to help you draw perpendicular lines in pencil.

2. On one of the 12" wide x 10 ½" high (30.5 cm x 26.7 cm) boards, draw diagonal lines from corner to corner *(see fig. 1)*. This will determine the center point of the front of the book.

3. Measure a rectangle 2" wide x 2 ½" high (5.1 cm x 6.4 cm) around the center point *(see fig. 2)*, making sure the rectangle is centered on the point (1 ¼" [3.2 cm] to the top and bottom of the center point, 1" [2.5 cm] to the left and right of the point). Draw the rectangle using your triangle to square things up.

4. On same boards, measure up two front spines, 2" wide x 10 ½" high (5.1 cm x 26.7 cm). Draw pencil lines for those.

5. Cut out boards with metal ruler and utility knife. Cut out window rectangle on front cover.

6. Measure and cut out two sheets of the decorative paper 13" wide x 12 ½" high (33 cm x 31.8 cm), making sure to square up the cuts against the paper's design, especially if it is geometric.

7. Lay paper decorative side down on a sheet of newsprint. Place front cover board on top of decorative paper, leaving 1" (2.5 cm) all around top, left, and bottom edges. The right edge should be flush with edge of decorative paper *(see fig. 3)*.

8. Brush a light coat of PVA glue onto wrong side of paper, making sure you cover the entire sheet. You will need to work fast because PVA glue sets up very quickly. (To slow the drying time, you may want to purchase some methyl cellulose and make a mixture of half methyl cellulose and half PVA.) Adhere paper to board and smooth out bubbles with edge of bone folder. Get out as many air bubbles as possible while doing this. It may look a little bumpy, but this should all smooth out as glue dries. You should burnish out as many wrinkles or major bumps as you can.

9. Using a craft knife on the paper corners, cut 45° angles on the top and bottom, and a square corner on the left edge corners *(see fig. 4)*.

10. Fold left edge of paper inward and burnish edge of book cover with bone folder. Brush on additional glue where needed and burnish flat. Do the same with the top and bottom edges.

11. With decorative paper face down on work surface, cut diagonals in front cover window *(see fig. 5)*. Brush on some glue and adhere to inside front cover. Burnish with bone folder.

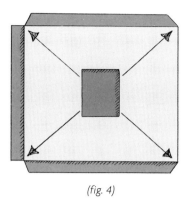

(fig. 4)

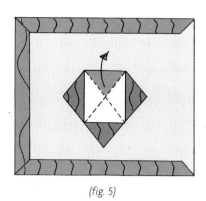

(fig. 5)

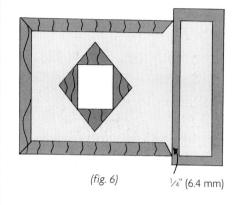

(fig. 6)　　　　　¼" (6.4 mm)

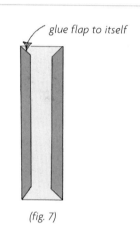

glue flap to itself

(fig. 7)

12. For back cover, lay paper decorative side down on a sheet of newsprint. Place back cover board on top of decorative paper, leaving 1" (2.5 cm) all around top, right, and bottom edges. The left edge should be flush with edge of decorative paper.

13. Repeat step eight for back cover.

14. Using a craft knife on the paper corners, cut 45° angles on the top and bottom, and a square corner on the right edge corners *(mirror image of fig. 4)*.

15. Fold right edge of paper inward and burnish edge of book cover with bone folder. Brush on additional glue where needed and burnish flat. Do the same with the top and bottom edges.

16. For front and back spines, measure out two pieces 3 ³⁄₄" wide x 12 ¹⁄₂" high (9.5 cm x 31.8 cm) of bookbinding fabric. Square up with triangle and cut out the pieces.

17. On cover board, measure in ³⁄₄" (1.9 cm) from left and draw a vertical pencil line, squaring up line with triangle.

18. Butt book cloth against pencil line, leaving 1" (2.5 cm) on top and 1" (2.5 cm) on the bottom of fabric. Brush glue onto the fabric and glue into place. Burnish with bone folder, making sure not to stab fabric with the pointy end. Do not fold in top and bottom edges yet.

19. Lay book cover face down and place spine board to the right of it, leaving a ¹⁄₄" (6.4 mm) gap between cover and spine *(see fig. 6)*. Make sure to leave the gap, otherwise the book cover will not open flat.

20. Brush glue onto the book cloth and adhere to spine board. Follow corner cutting technique discussed in step nine. Glue and burnish edges into inside front cover.

21. Attach a back spine board. On back cover board, measure in ³⁄₄" (1.9 cm) from right and draw a vertical pencil line, squaring up line with triangle.

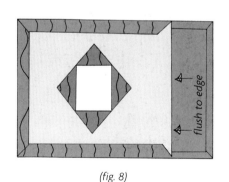

flush to edge

(fig. 8)

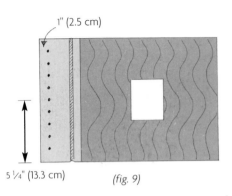

1" (2.5 cm)

5 ¼" (13.3 cm)

(fig. 9)

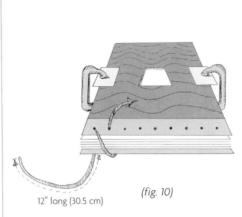

12" long (30.5 cm)

(fig. 10)

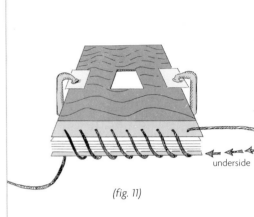

underside

(fig. 11)

22. Butt the book cloth against pencil line, leaving 1" (2.5 cm) on top and 1" (2.5 cm) on the bottom of the fabric. Brush some glue onto the fabric and glue into place. Burnish with bone folder, making sure not to stab fabric with the pointy end. Do not fold in top and bottom edges yet.

23. Lay book cover face down and place spine to the left of it, leaving a ¼" (6.4 mm) gap between cover and spine.

24. Brush glue onto the bookbinding fabric and adhere to spine. Follow corner cutting technique discussed in step nine. Glue and burnish edges into inside front cover. Using point of bone folder, push fabric down into the gaps between spines and covers.

25. For spine end papers, cut two 2 ½" x 10 ½" (6.4 cm x 26.7 cm) rectangles out of the book cloth. Fold fabric in ½" (1.3 cm) on the top and bottom and glue to fabric itself *(see fig. 7)*. Lay book cover decorative side down. Butt fabric against inner edge of binding fabric, leaving ½" (1.3 cm) top and bottom. Glue into place and burnish *(see fig. 8)*.

26. Repeat process for back spine end paper.

27. For endsheets, cut out 11 ¾" wide x 10" high (29.8 cm x 25.4 cm) sheet of decorative paper for the inside cover. Lay one sheet decorative side up on inside front cover. Flip board over and raw a pencil outline of the window. Cut out window. Brush on glue and place ¼" (6.4 mm) in from top, bottom, and left edges and flush with right cover edge, making sure paper window aligns with cardboard cover window. Repeat process for back inside cover, leaving off the window step.

28. For inside pages, measure ten 10" x 14" (25.4 cm x 35.6 cm) sheets of watercolor paper. Mark *very lightly* with a pencil. Place the metal ruler to the left of pencil line as you would if you were going to trim out the pages with a craft knife. Instead, put pressure on your ruler with your left hand. With your right hand tear the page along the ruler edge from top to bottom, forming a deckled edge. Erase any visible pencil lines with a white eraser.

29. Stack and straighten pages as best you can and place in book, centering from top to bottom, but running flush with spine.

30. Measure and draw a vertical pencil line 1" (2.5 cm) in from the left edge of your cover. Make a tick mark at the vertical center of that line, at 5 ¼" (13.3 cm). Make four tick marks to the bottom of the center point, 1 ⅛" (2.9 cm) apart. Then make four tick marks to the top of the center point, 1 ⅛" (2.9 cm) apart, for a total of nine tick marks (see fig. 9).

31. Straighten the pages and cover, and C-clamp the spine of book onto the edge of a wooden board. You may want to place a piece of paper or cardboard between your clamps and your cover to protect the paper.

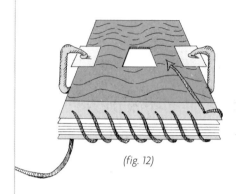

(fig. 12)

32. Drill holes at each of the tick marks, going straight through all the layers of the book and through the back cover. Unclamp and erase pencil line with a white eraser.

33. Take 3 yards (2.7 m) of ribbon and sew on a 6" (15.2 cm) length of thread to the end. Start sewing book binding as follows: Starting at hole one, run ribbon through the bottom of book and out through the top of hole one leaving 12" (30.5 cm) of ribbon hanging off end. Wrap ribbon around spine and proceed up through hole two (see fig. 10). Repeat this process through all the holes until you've come to hole nine. At that point, wrap ribbon around outside of the bottom of the spine to underside of hole nine (see fig. 11). Pass the needle and ribbon up through (see fig. 12). While you do this, make sure you do not split the ribbon that is already in the hole. Splitting the ribbon can happen easily, but can be avoided by pulling the ribbon currently in the hole to the side as you pass the needle and ribbon through a second time. Wrap the ribbon over the spine, forming a criss-cross with the ribbon that has already been sewn. Proceed to the underside of hole eight, pulling the ribbon up through hole eight (see fig. 13). Continue this same process through all the holes until you are back at hole one. Wrap remaining ribbon around top of the spine and tie the two ends in a bow (see fig. 14).

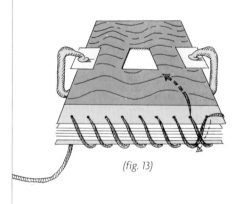

(fig. 13)

34. Trim ends of ribbon by folding vertically in half and cutting a 45° angle. This will give your ends a dart in the middle.

35. Place photos in book with photo corners.

TIP Keep a kitchen towel handy during this project. When burnishing the bubbles and wrinkles out of the paper, glue can seep from the seams. Use the towel to wipe up the excess glue immediately to prevent damaging the decorative paper.

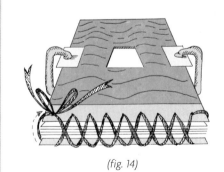

(fig. 14)

Zen Centerpiece

SLEEK BAMBOO GARDEN

MATERIALS

One shallow square dish

Heavy metal flower frog

Three protea flowers

Seven tall, curly
fresh bamboo stems

Gardening shears

Gray river pebbles,
enough to cover the
bottom of the dish
and the metal frog

A miniature forest of green bamboo on each table creates a sleek and serene décor that projects a modern simplicity. By using only two types of plants set in a shallow bowl of glossy river stones, you manufacture a relaxing and lush table setting. Curly bamboo is long lasting and fast growing. The tall stalks have fantastic coils in the stems and satiny dark green leaves that add a mild texture to the centerpiece. It takes some force to settle the stems into a metal frog, but once in place and watered, they will last for a long time, and certainly won't wilt during the day or evening. The centerpiece should not block guests' view, so place it judiciously, or make a version people can peer over.

1. Cut the bottoms of the curly bamboo down to about 24" (61 cm), varying the heights slightly to fit the curly gnarls into one another.

2. Place the bamboo into the center of the frog. Secure to frog by piercing the bottom of the stems with the needles of the frog.

3. Cut the bottoms of the protea, and score the bottom edges of the stems with the shears, so they fit into the frog needles. Place on the outside edges of the frog around the bamboo.

4. Fill the dish with rocks, covering the frog and the bottom. Fill with water.

TIP *If you have a difficult time settling the bamboo stalks into a metal frog, pierce the bottom of the stalk with a small nail. Don't make a big hole, just an indention to guide the frog points.*

MATERIALS

Natural sugar
(sandy color)

Two interior
gardening pebbles

One sheet ¹/₈" (3 mm)
thick balsa wood, cut
down to 4" wide × 6"
high (10.2 cm × 15.2 cm)

One strip of
¹/₂" × ¹/₂"
(1.3 cm × 1.3 cm)
balsa wood

Black semigloss
latex paint

Small paintbrush

Mitre box

Small saw

Wood glue

Small rattan rake

Ruler

Drafting triangle, 45°

Pencil

Sandpaper

Wood filler

A Garden of One's Own

ZEN ROCK GARDEN

Is the food too good to play with during dinner? Perhaps there's a long time between courses. A Zen rock garden is the toy for fidgety fingers or pauses in conversation. Every time you rake the surface, you create a new work of art. We filled our gardens with natural, unbleached sugar, so it looks like sand, but won't be gritty if a little winds up in the food. (And you can't guarantee against that when there is champagne to be had.) Set one garden at each place setting, or place one between settings, so people share the Zen experience. Rake the surface and place the pebbles before guests arrive. A perfect accompaniment to the Zen bamboo garden (see page 268), pair these decorations with a bamboo placemat, sand-colored dishes, and chopsticks.

1. Measure two strips of the ½" x ½" (1.3 cm x 1.3 cm) balsa wood to 6" (15.2 cm). Place a tick mark with pencil at 6" (15.2 cm). With the triangle, draw a line 45° inward from the 6" (15.2 cm) tick mark. Do this on both ends. Place in mitre box and cut, leaving a small allowance for the saw blade.

2. Measure two strips of the ½" x ½" (1.3 cm x 1.3 cm) balsa wood to 4" (10.2 cm). Place a tick mark with pencil at 4" (10.2 cm). With the triangle, draw a line 45° inward from the 4" (10.2 cm) tick mark. Do this on both ends. Place in mitre box and cut, once again leaving a small allowance for the saw blade.

3. Place 4" (10.2 cm) pieces and 6" (15.2 cm) pieces on top of the ⅛" x 4" x 6" (3 mm x 10.2 cm x 15.2 cm) rectangle you cut in step one, creating a framework around the outer edges.

4. Make sure mitred edges fit together nicely, you may have to do a little sanding to make them meet exactly.

5. Glue framework onto 4" x 6" (10.2 cm x 15.2 cm) base and let glue set about 20 minutes.

6. Fill any cracks with wood filler and let that set about ½ hour.

7. Sand lightly to remove any extra wood filler or rough edges on balsa wood.

8. Paint it black and let it dry 1 hour.

9. Fill with natural sugar and rocks.

10. Make a design around the rocks with either the rake or a pencil.

11. Place rake in the sugar-sand and place the garden on the table.

VARIATION *The mini garden can double as a place card holder. Print out the names, and nestle them into the sugar-sand. But if you prefer the rock garden to be amusing instead of useful, use silk "fortune cookies" as place cards. Write each name on a scroll of paper and place in the cookie.*

Toying with Guests
WIND-UP NAME CARDS

Normally place cards don't move. These do…when you wind them up and let them loose on the table. In a sly reference to formal wear, wind-up penguins or monkeys are an amusing and charming injection of fun. A kitsch element like a wind-up toy relies on the guests' knowledge of your personality and humor. If everyone thinks of you as the epitome of refinement—whether correct or not—they may think the style doesn't quite match. However, if your style is relaxed and modern, these toys will be a huge hit.

DIRECTIONS FOR THE MONKEY GIRLS

1. Cut a 3" (7.6 cm) strip of faux pearl ribbon. Shape pearls around head of monkey. Glue into place using the cotton swabs.

2. Trim off row of pearls from back of veil. Add a daisy to the hand and wrap wire at least two times around wrist of monkey. Secure wire end and cut with scissors.

3. Use your favorite computer layout software to inset each guest name in an oval $3/4$" wide x $1/2$" high (1.9 cm x 1.3 cm). For a decorative element, you can add a tilde underneath the name.

4. Print the names.

5. Cut out the ovals and dab a little glue on the back of the paper. Adhere to belly of the monkey girl.

VARIATION *For a slightly different look along the same lines, use different wind-up creatures. Frogs will give a funnier look to a place setting. Robots will give a futuristic look.*

MATERIALS

Miniature wind up toys, about 2" tall (5.1 cm)

Personal computer

Printer

Your favorite computer layout software

Bright white inkjet or laser paper

Guest list

$1/4$" (6.4 mm) black ribbon

2" (5.1 cm) translucent wire ribbon with faux pearls on edges

Party favor daisies

Roundstone sequins

PVA or craft glue

Cotton swabs

Scissors

DIRECTIONS FOR THE MONKEY BOYS

1. Cut an 8" (20.3 cm) strip of black ribbon. Tie a bow around the monkey neck. Trim ends on a diagonal with scissors.

2. Glue a roundstone sequin to each of the monkey ears.

3. Repeat step three and four from the monkey girl directions.

4. Cut out the ovals with scissors and dab a little glue on the back. Adhere to belly of the monkey boy.

DIRECTIONS FOR THE EMPIRE PENGUIN GIRLS

1. Cut a 3" (7.6 cm) strip of faux pearl ribbon. Shape pearls around head of penguin. Glue into place using the cotton swabs.

2. Trim off row of pearls from back of veil. Add two roundstone sequins vertically about $1/4$" (6.4 mm) under penguin girl's beak.

3. Use your favorite computer layout software to inset each guest name in a rectangle $3/4$" wide x $1/2$" high (1.9 cm x 1.3 cm). We used 9 point Bernhard Tango typeface for ours. For a decorative element, you can add a tilde underneath the name.

4. Print the names.

5. Cut out the rectangles with scissors and dab a little glue on the back. We cut a little diagonal in the name card to make it look like it was going under her arm. Adhere next to the wing of the penguin girl.

DIRECTIONS FOR THE EMPIRE PENGUIN BOYS

1. Cut an 8" (20.3 cm) strip of black ribbon. Tie a bow around the penguin neck. Trim ends on a diagonal with scissors.

2. Using a cotton swab, glue two roundstone sequins vertically under the bow tie.

3. Use your favorite computer layout software to inset each guest name in a rectangle $3/4$" wide x $1/2$" high (1.9 cm x 1.3 cm). We used 9 point Bernhard Tango typeface for ours. For a decorative element, you can add a tilde underneath the name.

4. Print the names.

5. Cut out the rectangles with scissors and dab a little glue on the back. We cut a little diagonal in the name card to make it look like it was going under his arm. Adhere to the wing of the penguin boy.

MATERIALS

8" (20.3 cm), 11" (27.9 cm),
14" (35.6 cm) hatboxes

Six sheets of 20" × 30"
(50.8 cm × 76.2 cm)
decorative paper
(allow two sheets
for each tier)

Spray adhesive

Craft knife

Bone folder

Daisy combo packet of
rubber flowers

Black-and-white
photocopy of a couple
in wedding attire

Black-and-white
photocopy of you and
your spouse's faces
to fit onto wedding
couple image

8" × 10 1/4"
(20.3 cm × 26 cm)
black foam core

Small paper flowers
for party favors

One box
roundstone sequins

One packet
rhinestones
1/2" (1.3 cm) and
5/8" (1.6 cm)

1/2 yard (.5 m)
netting or tulle

Craft glue

Pencil

Tiers of Joy

WEDDING CAKE CARD BOX

Card boxes are not a necessity, but many couples use them to assure that cards and messages stay together and safe. Because guests do not always bring gifts and cards to a reception, it is a good idea to place a card box, or indeed a gift table, in a non-prominent position. Even though you don't want gifts to take center stage, you can still go vivid. Think outside the box—or at least re-shape it—and appropriate a standard image for a different purpose.

1. Top tier: Take off lid of 8" (20.3 cm) hatbox (the lid will not be used in the final project). Trace around lid shape onto back side of top tier paper. Start cutting, leaving about 3/4" (1.9 cm) extra all around as you cut. Final circle size should be around 9" (22.9 cm) in diameter.

2. Spray adhesive onto back of circle and center on bottom of 8" (20.3 cm) hatbox. Smooth out bumps with a bone folder. Press extra paper over edges and smooth with bone folder, flattening as best you can the small creases that happen as the paper wraps around the circular shape. Flip the box bottom side up. This will now be the top of the cake.

3. Measure the depth of the sides of the circular box. The top tier shown measured 3 1/2" (8.9 cm). Add 3/4" (1.9 cm) to the depth, to allow enough paper to tuck to the inside of the box. Cut that dimension out of the second piece of paper along the entire length of the paper.

VARIATION *If your wedding will be more traditional than funky, look for papers, or even fabrics, that match your style. Remnants of silk georgette with accents of lace look very beautiful in the cake form. You can also find inexpensive buttons and hot glue them to the box, making Victorian stylized flower clusters.*

Ours was 4 ¼" x 30" (10.8 cm x 76.2 cm). Spray adhesive on the back side of the paper and adhere it to the box, butting the paper edge against the top of the "cake" and tucking the extra ³⁄₄" (1.9 cm) of paper into the inside of the box. Smooth with bone folder.

4. Middle tier: Select second tier paper style. Take the lid off the 11" (27.9 cm) hatbox. Discard the lid. Follow the instructions for top tier, measuring the depth of the sides and adding ³⁄₄" (1.9 cm) extra for tucking in edges. If paper does not make the circumference of the box, add another strip, matching design as best you can.

5. Bottom tier: Take the lid off the 14" (35.6 cm) hatbox. Keep the lid. Cut a 6 ³⁄₄" x ¼" (17.1 cm x 6.4 mm) slit 1 ¼" (3.2 cm) in from the edge of the lid. This will be the slit for the cards. Place a sheet of decorative paper on the work surface, right side down. Place the lid on top and trace around it with a pencil. Cut out the shape, leaving a ³⁄₄" (1.9 cm) allowance all around. Spray adhesive onto the back side of the paper and cover top of hatbox lid, tucking the ³⁄₄" (1.9 cm) extra over the lid edge. Burnish with bone folder. Flip lid over and cut out paper from slit with a craft knife.

6. Measure depth of lid side and then add ³⁄₄" (1.9 cm) to tuck under the rim. Cut out strip and spray mount to lid side, butting top edge of paper against top edge of lid. Fold extra paper to underside of lid and burnish. If the paper is not big enough to cover the entire circumference of the box, add another strip, matching the design as best you can.

7. Measure depth of box. This time add 1 ½" (3.8 cm) extra to depth for folding inside box and onto bottom. Spray adhesive to the underside of the paper and burnish onto the side of the box, leaving ³⁄₄" (1.9 cm) to fold over the top of the box and ³⁄₄" (1.9 cm) on the bottom. Burnish with bone folder, folding in top edges and folding under bottom edges.

8. Place the lid on the bottom tier.

9. When decorating the box, you can do just about anything you want. We followed the concept of a traditional cake, but made it livelier to match the colorful pattern. We pasted the little flowers around the top tier and then glued the ½" (1.3 cm) rhinestones to the flower centers. Paste roundstones on a glue strip arc forming swags around the cake.

10. Because the second tier is larger than the top, use bigger flowers and the $^3/_4$" (1.9 cm) rhinestones in the center of the flowers. Repeat the roundstone swags of the first tier and make edging around the top and bottom of this tier with the roundstone sequins. Paste rhinestones around the paper. In our example, we placed them in the bottom squares of the tier.

11. Use the biggest flowers on the third tier and glue the $^3/_4$" (1.9 cm) rhinestones in the center of each flower. In the example shown, we glued the decorations to the lid. Glue roundstones in swags around the tier.

12. For the bride and groom, spray mount the bride and groom image to a piece of foam core. Cut out the shape of couple. Leave about $^1/_2$" (1.3 cm) strip at their feet. Make sure the strip is square, so the bride and groom will stand up straight, not leaning to one side. Measure the width of the base of the bride and groom. Add $^1/_2$" (1.3 cm) to that dimension and cut out a strip of foam core that long by 1" (2.5 cm) high. Out of the center of that strip, cut a channel $^1/_4$" (6.4 mm) high by the width of the bride and groom figure. Insert bride and groom feet first into the stand and adhere together with craft glue.

13. With pencil point, stab a hole in the bride's hands where the bouquet will be. Place three paper flowers in the hole and pull the wires through to the back of foam core. Twist wire so flowers don't fall out.

14. Obviously, you won't have any wedding pictures of yourselves at this point. Cut out the faces of the black-and-white photocopies of you and your fiancé. Glue them to the wedding portrait. Add a few roundstone sequins to the headpiece and glue the bride and groom to the top tier of the cake.

15. Glue the three tiers together at each of the bases. Top with a 26" (66 cm) piece of netting folded in half to 13" (33 cm). You can secure this by placing a few straight pins through the netting into the heads of the bride and groom.

TIP *One strip of paper may not be enough to cover each hatbox. You may need to use extra strips of paper and match up the design.*

Chapel of Love
SACRED TABLE TOPPER

There's something satisfying about appropriating a standard *Saturday Evening Post* image for decorative purposes. A chapel in a field and a couple speeding away in a "Just Married" convertible recall an archetype of love and marriage. It becomes half humor and half homage. More often than not, reality looks very different from this idyllic image. That's really part of the fun. If you were getting married in a country chapel and speeding away in a convertible, this centerpiece would seem oddly self-referential. But, for other styles of weddings, this centerpiece is amusing and calls up the idea of a wedding in general and the free feeling of speeding away with your sweetheart.

1. Place 11" x 11" (27.9 cm x 27.9 cm) piece of faux grass directly on top of 11" x 11" (27.9 cm x 27.9 cm) square of floral styrofoam.

2. Make a hole under the grass, about 3" (7.6 cm) from what will be the back and 5 ½" (14 cm) from the left of the square. Place the cord for the wreath lights through the hole. Lift up grass and run the cord of the wreath lights under the grass and out what will become the back of the centerpiece. Leave about 6" (15.2 cm) of cord with the batteries hanging out of the back of the piece.

TIP *Real sod and real flowers can be substituted for the faux grass and party favor daisies. The picket fences can be painted white before assembling. If there are any bald spots in the real grass, add 2" (5.1 cm) of floral wire into the hole and attach one of the sprigs you've removed to make room for the church.*

MATERIALS

11" × 11" × 1 ½" thick (27.9 cm × 27.9 cm × 3.8 cm) piece of floral styrofoam

Six pieces 5 ½" wide × 4 ½" high (14 cm × 11.4 cm) dollhouse fencing

11" × 11" (27.9 cm × 27.9 cm) square of faux grass

Fifteen party favor daisies

One 8 ½" × 11" (21.6 cm × 27.9 cm) piece of black craft foam sheeting

One scale train accessory model church

One scale train accessory bride and groom

One matchbox-size convertible car

One battery-operated set of wreath lights

2 yards (1.8 m) of 1 ½" wide (3.8 cm) lime green cotton ribbon

Small glass votive holder

Wood glue

Superglue

Floral wire

Fifteen to twenty medium-sized household nails

Personal computer and printer (optional)

Utility knife

Ruler

Drafting triangle

Two straight pins or needles and lime green thread

3. Measure and cut fencing to run around three sides of square foam and grass, making sure edges of fencing butt against each other closely. Weave floral wire in and out of the bottom of the fencing uprights.

4. Secure fencing and wire to styrofoam by pushing household nails through the woven wire into the styrofoam. Do this all around the bottom of the fencing until it feels tight and secure.

5. Glue the butted edges of the fence with wood glue.

6. Measure and cut a 2 ½" wide x 7 ½" long (6.4 cm x 19.1 cm) strip of black craft foam. This will be your road.

7. Clear a path for the road by pulling out some grass sprigs. Start at center front of centerpiece and work your way to back of square until you have cleared a path approximately 2 ½" wide x 6" long (6.4 cm x 15.2 cm).

8. Place your road on the centerpiece, leaving approximately 1 ½" (3.8 cm) protruding in front.

9. Wrap a ribbon all the way around the edges of the styrofoam bottom, starting and ending at center back. Cut the ribbon, leaving ½" (1.3 cm) extra to tuck under. Tuck under edge and secure to styrofoam using the straight pins. (You could also handstitch this if you want.)

10. Tuck protruding part of road under ribbon in front.

11. Assemble church model using instructions in kit, but don't mount it to base provided in kit.

12. Temporarily place the church at the end of the road. Pull out sprigs of grass to accommodate the base of the church, because you'll want the church to be nestled in the grass. Set the church aside.

13. Stuff wreath lights into votive holder. Turn votive holder upside down and place in the nesting place you've just created for the church.

14. Place church on top of votive and nestle it into the grass.

15. Cut figurines of wedding couple in half with utility knife, so they sit nicely in the car. Superglue into place.

16. Using your favorite computer layout software, make a miniature "Just Married" sign to place on the back of the car. Print out the sign. Cut out and glue onto back of car.

17. Place car on road.

18. Place party favor daisies randomly on grass and stick stems through styrofoam.

19. Place batteries in wreath lights, turn on the switch, and watch your church glow.

Sticky Guest Book

iZONE BOOKLET FOR EACH TABLE

MATERIALS

Personal computer

Your favorite computer layout software

Printer

Bright white inkjet or laser paper

Light pink inkjet or laser paper

Spray mount adhesive

Cellophane tape

Corrugated, wavy silver paper

Silver cord with tassels

iZone camera and adhesive film

Drafting triangle, 45°

Metal ruler

Bone folder

Craft knife

Template from page 295

Let's face it: guest books can be beautiful, but dead boring. Sorry, it's true. Liven it up a little and let your favorite people's creativity show with mini guest books on each table. Leave a booklet, an iZone camera, sticky film, and scissors on the table. Your guests are sure to take the most charming photos of each other living it up in celebration of you two. Instead of empty pages, give guests a head start with a rectangle to frame each photo and lines for the message. (After the third toast of the evening, lines will be helpful, indeed.)

1. Using your favorite computer layout software, create a document 4 ½" wide x 10" tall (11.4 cm x 25.4 cm). On one-half of the document, create a bordered box that measures 1 ½" wide x 1 ⅛" high (3.8 cm x 2.9 cm). Put the words "Place picture here" in the center of the box. Under the box, make several horizontal rules and some type that reads, "Wishes for the couple." Copy this layout onto the other half of the document and print it. Print six copies of this and trim to size.

2. Spray mount two of the sheets back to back until you have three back-to-back sheets. Fold sheets in half width-wise. Unfold and stack the sheets, so they will nest in each other when folded.

3. Create another page with the same dimensions and set some type that reads, "Guests," 2" (5.1 cm) from the top of the page and centered on one-half of the document on the right-hand side. Print on the light pink paper and trim. Fold in half and score with bone folder. Place in front of pages created in step one, so it will make the first and last pages of the book.

4. Photocopy the template from page 295 and tape on three sides to the back of the corrugated paper. Cut along straight lines and score along dotted lines. Cut out front window.

5. Using the bone folder, fold cover in half along score lines.

6. Place interior pages in book and tie into place with silver cord. Make a knot on the outside of book on the center of the spine.

7. Place one at each table with an iZone Polaroid camera, extra sticky film, scissors, and a pen.

Kiddie Confections

LOLLIPOP BOUQUET

Kids need a little extra fun at weddings. With all the adults gabbing and dancing, kids have a tendency to feel left out or restless. Keeping the younger guests happy and entertained keeps everyone else happy. A lollipop bouquet makes children part of the wedding itself, by taking a standard wedding icon and making it fun—that is, full of sugar. Yes, the sweets will enhance any hyperactivity, but if the adults are imbibing in their vices, why can't the kids? If you want a dramatic look, bundle a bunch of red lollipops in a lace collar. Ours reflects a garden theme, with silk leaves and marzipan fruits.

1. Attach 2" (5.1 cm) of floral wire to the end of each lollipop stick, wrapping it onto stick with white floral tape. Round out the lollipop wrappers with scalloped-edged scissors. Pierce popsicle sticks into back side of marzipan. Don't push sticks all the way through the candy.

2. Create a bouquet with the eight silk leaves, assembling them in a circle. Place all the lollipops and pinwheels into the center of the leaves in this order: three big lollipops in the back, four rectangular lollipops in the middle, three marzipan fruits in front, and two pinwheels on the right-hand side. Place two more rectangular lollipops behind the three large lollipops in the back to round out the bouquet.

3. Wrap base of stems with floral wire or floral tape to secure bouquet, if needed. Wrap the ribbon around the stems. Wrap the stems with enough ribbon to hide the floral wire and tape and tie off the end. Knot ribbon or wrap decoratively.

4. We placed the end of the ribbon below the calla lily leaves. Wrap the ribbon over the end of the stems and up the opposite side. Wrap ribbon around the stem, all the way down to the end. The stem should be covered. Knot ribbon or wrap decoratively.

5. With the ribbon in front, flip the ribbon up at an angle, exposing the reverse color and anchoring the ribbon in place with Superglue. Leave time for it to dry before flipping the ribbon back on itself, still in an upward angle. Anchor again. Trim end at an angle.

TIP *Use Saf-T-Pops for little kids if you worry that they will run around with lollipops in their mouths. For older kids, you can use dulled pins to hold the ribbon, otherwise, use Superglue.*

MATERIALS

Three pieces of marzipan fruits

Six multicolored rectangular lollipops

Three big round multicolored lollipops

Eight silk calla lily leaves

One roll of two-sided ribbon

Three popsicle sticks

Toys, like the pinwheels we used here

White floral tape

Green floral wire

Dulled straight pins

Superglue

Scalloped-edged decorative scissors

Where Do I Sit?

MINIATURE SEAT ASSIGNMENTS

MATERIALS FOR TABLE ASSIGNMENT

Miniature dollhouse tables

Miniature dollhouse chairs

Personal computer and printer

Your favorite computer layout software

8 1/2" × 11" (21.6 cm × 27.9 cm) colored stationery paper

Letter and number beads

Decorative beads

Tacks or brads

Beading wire

Bone folder

Craft knife

There's always a bit of excitement at the beginning of a reception when guests discover who their tablemates are. It's not uncommon to see calligraphied posters beautifully directing people to their appointed positions. Beautiful handwriting is one option; smart imagery is another. These miniature tables and chairs direct people in a charming and amusing way. Atop each miniature table, place a folded card listing the guests that will sit together at one table. Arrange the miniatures on the seat assignment table. Mark each person's position at their actual tables with their name resting on a miniature chair.

DIRECTIONS FOR TABLE ASSIGNMENT

1. Using your favorite computer layout software, create a 3" (7.6 cm) square for each table. Set the guests' names for each table in the bottom half of the squares. (The cards will be folded so you will only see part of each card).

2. Print onto your stationery paper and trim to size. Fold in half and score with bone folder.

3. String up three beads on your wire and then add letter beads to spell "TABLE 1," "TABLE 2," and so on. Place a single bead between "TABLE" and the number. Follow with three beads.

4. Hammer a brad into the underside of the left and right ends of front edge of table. Wrap the wire around brads and string along front.

5. Place card on table top. Place each card-topped miniature on the seating assignment table.

DIRECTIONS FOR SEATING ASSIGNMENT

1. Using your favorite computer layout software, create a 1 1/2" high x 1 1/4" wide (3.8 cm x 3.2 cm) square for each chair. Set each guest's name in the bottom half of the square, one name to a square. (The cards will be folded so you will only read the bottom part of each card). Print and trim.

2. Fold in half and score with bone folder. Place each card on a miniature chair. Place the card-topped chair on each plate or at the head of each plate in dining area.

Mini Frame To Go

PLACE CARD FRAME IN ORGANDY SACK

Place cards don't have to be disposable. A small frame with its own organdy sack serves as a beautiful place card during the reception. By dressing up a basic metal frame and with a little decoration, you provide a nice keepsake of the day. A small organdy sack not only ties the look into the rest of the décor, but makes it a take-away treasure.

Small, inexpensive frames and organdy bags can be found in most craft or card stores. If you have a prominent color scheme, buy the bags and decorations in both colors. Use one color for the roundstone sequins and the opposite color for the sack. If you don't want to over-coordinate, use the same color for both elements, for a subtler look.

1. With your favorite computer layout software, create a document that is 3 $\frac{1}{4}$" wide x 2 $\frac{1}{4}$" high (8.3 cm x 5.7 cm). You can also set up eight of these in an 8 $\frac{1}{4}$" x 11" (21 cm x 27.9 cm) document, two across and four down.

2. Type in guest's name, set in your favorite typeface, and center on page.

3. Print on colored stationery paper.

4. Cut out and insert in frame.

5. Glue roundstones on frame corners.

6. Place bag on plate or at the head of the place setting. Then place frame on bag. Guests can take the frames home in the little sacks.

VARIATION *Instead of printing guests' names, you can add a special touch with calligraphy. You can hire a calligrapher to make up the cards. Double-check the spelling of the guests' names before you give the artist the list and after the cards have been finished.*

Templates

Great free art you can copy directly from this book

Swatch Us Get Hitched, page 52

You're Invited

Tea and Camaraderie, page 64

12-349

HOTEL D'AMORE GUEST

WHO:

WHAT:

WHEN:

WHERE:

reception to follow

12-349

HOTEL D'AMORE GUEST

WILL ATTEND

WILL NOT ATTEND

please respond by

Where in the World?, page 68

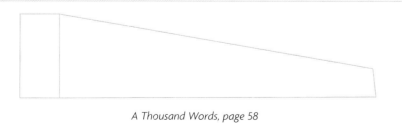

A Thousand Words, page 58

Curvy embrace, page 34

Blossoming Thanks template
page 26

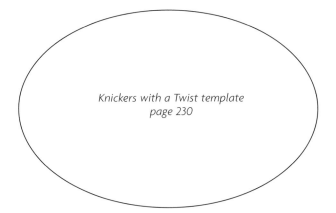

Knickers with a Twist template
page 230

Guest Survival Kit
page 224

Maybe, Baby! template, page 234, enlarge to 105%

Sticky Guest Book template, page 284, enlarge to 125%

Guests

[paste photo here]

[paste photo here]

wishes for the couple:

wishes for the couple:

Henna Party templates, page 160

Reflection of Love template, page 156

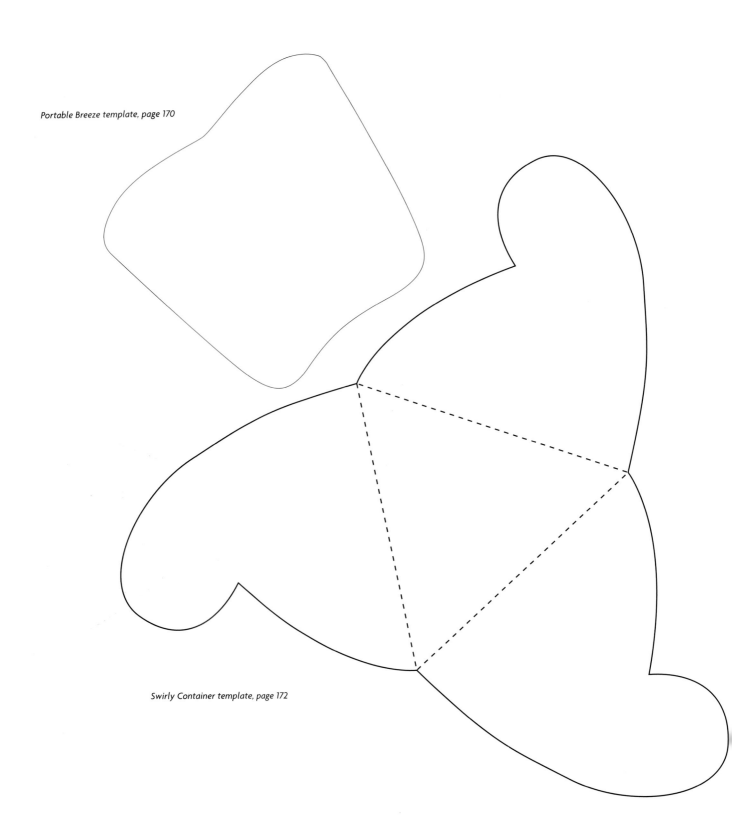

Portable Breeze template, page 170

Swirly Container template, page 172

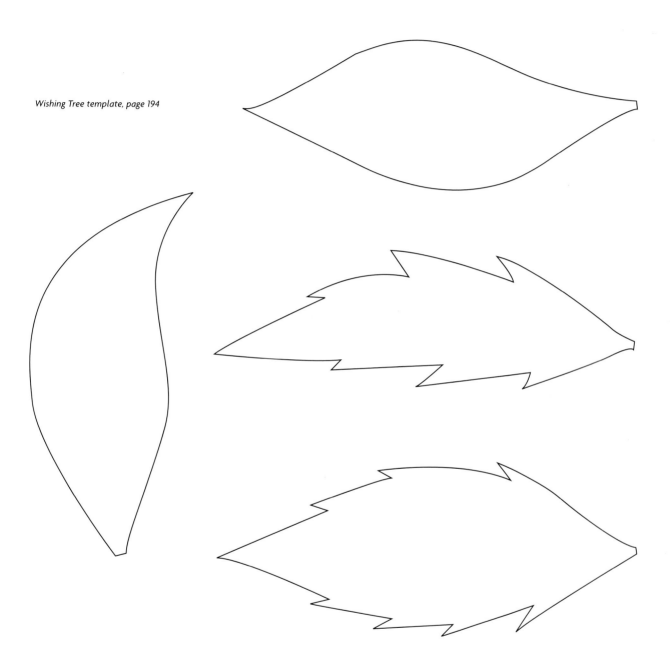

Wishing Tree template, page 194

Artists' Directory

Project Credits

Carolynn DeCillo
pages 236, 294

Mary Newell Depalma
pages 216, 217, 219, 246, 250, 254, 255

Kimberly Gray
page 72

Andrea Renzi McFadden
pages 36, 46

Christine Traulich
www.redbliss.com
page 70

Lynne Waring
page 67

Calligraphy Artists

Nan DeLuca
New York, NY 10012 USA
Telephone: (212) 477-3732
Fax: (425) 969-8667
deluca212@aol.com
pages 98, 100

Melissa Dinwiddie
Melissa Dinwiddie Designworks
Palo Alto, CA 94303 USA
Telephone: (650) 325-7687
Fax: (650) 325-2615
www.mddesignworks.com and
  www.melissaink.com
info@mddesignworks.com
pages 79, 82, 84, 91, 93, 133, 134, 139

Lisa J. Kennedy
LJK Calligraphy
Rowley, MA 01969 USA
Telephone: (978) 948-5434
www.usabride.com/wed/calligraphy
ljkraffi@gis.net
page 136

Bette Matthews
Brooklyn, NY 11217 USA
Telephone/Fax: (718) 857-4699
BetteMatthews@aol.com
pages 87, 91, 105, 127, 139

Susan L. Ramsey
Calligraphic Creations
Norwalk, CT 06851 USA
Telephone/Fax: (203) 847-5715
www.callig.com
Calligraphic@aol.com
pages 97, 100, 102, 107, 109, 111, 127, 129

Christopher J. Watkins
Watkins and Watkins Artisans, Inc.
Pickens, SC 29671 USA
Telephone/Fax: 864-878-1357
www.watkinsandwatkins.com
watkins-watkins@mindspring.com
page 129

Hilary Williams
Hil-Ink Calligraphy
North Hollywood, CA 91602 USA
Telephone: (818) 760-3406
Fax: (818) 760-3912
www.hil-ink.com
hilary@hil-ink.com
pages 80, 89, 115, 118, 120, 125, 127, 129

Beverly Wladkowski
B Creative
Ijamsville, MD 21754 USA
Telephone/Fax: (301) 831-6004
www.bcreativecalligraphy.com
bwladkowski@bcreativecalligraphy.com
pages 116, 123

Photographers

Bobbie Bush Photography
www.bobbiebush.com

Brian Piper Photography
West Chester, PA

Resources

A.C. Moore
www.acmoore.com

A.I. Friedman
44 West 18th Street
New York, NY 10011 USA
Telephone: (212) 243-9000
Fax: (212) 242-1238
Calligraphy, art supplies, books, stationery items, fine papers, ribbon, frames, mat board

The Angelgrove Tree Seed Company
Mission, KS 66202 USA
Telephone: (913) 362-7864
www.spencerian.com or
    www.trees-seeds.com
michael@spencerian.com
Seeds to use for the bonsai project

Association for the Calligraphic Arts
1223 Woodward Avenue
South Bend, IN 46616 USA
Telephone: (219) 233-6233
Fax: (219) 233-6229
www.calligraphicarts.org
aca@calligraphicarts.org

Bead Works
23 Church Street
Cambridge, MA 02138 USA
Telephone: (617) 868-9777
and
1076 Boylston Street
Boston, MA 02215 USA
Telephone: (617) 247-7227
www.beadworksboston.com
From tiny seed beads in vibrant colors to gigantic semi-precious beads, this store is likely to have it—as well as a supply of tools to finish the beading projects.

Black Ink
5 Brattle Street, Harvard Square
Cambridge, MA 02138 USA
Telephone: (617) 497-1221
and
101 Charles Street
Boston, MA 02114 USA
Telephone: (617) 723-3883

Black Ink Home
370 Broadway
Cambridge, MA 02139 USA
Telephone: (617) 576-0707
Black Ink, and its spin-off of larger goods, ceramics, and furniture called Black Ink Home, are a treasure trove of inspiring and useful items. From "sushi-pops" to lunch boxes and bowling-ball patches, the genius behind these stores collects the best of what's out there—kitsch, industrial, and elegant— for the customers who outfit their homes and projects with their goodies.

Charles Ro Supply Co.
662 Cross Street
Malden, MA 02148 USA
Telephone: (781) 321-0090
www.charlesro.com

eBay
www.ebay.com
Want toys, vases, vintage Girl Scout patches, or anything else you can't seem to find in stores? Check eBay.

The Fabric Place
Telephone: (800) 556-3700
www.fabricplace.com

GetSuckered.com
www.getsuckered.com
Candy-making supplies, molds, and luster and pearl dust.

The Great Wind-Up
93 Pike Street #201
Seattle, WA 98101 USA
Telephone: (206) 621-9370
www.greatwindup.com
Wind-up and tin toys

HobbyCraft
Head Office
Bournemouth
United Kingdom
44 1202 596 100
Stores throughout the UK

JoAnn Fabrics
www.joann.com

John Lewis
Flagship Store
Oxford
London W1A 1EX
United Kingdom
44 11 20 7269 7711
Stores throughout the UK

John Neal Bookseller
1833 Spring Garden Street
Greensboro, NC 27403 USA
Telephone: (336) 272-6139 or
(800) 369-9598 (Toll free in USA
and Canada)
Fax: (336) 272-9015
www.johnnealbooks.com
info@johnnealbooks.com
Calligraphy, art supplies, books, fine papers, rubber stamp and embossing supplies

Kate's Paperie
561 Broadway
New York, NY 10012-3918 USA
Telephone: (212) 941-9816
www.katespaperie.com
info@katespaperie.com
Fine papers, stationery items, ribbon, hand-made paper boxes and bags, rubber stamp and embossing supplies, pressed flowers

Ken McCallister's Art Supplies
500 Salem Avenue
Dayton, OH 45406 USA
Telephone: (937) 278-0844
Calligraphy and art supplies, fine papers

Letter Arts Review
P. O. Box 9986
Greensboro, NC 27429 USA
Telephone (336) 272-6139 or (800) 348-PENS (Toll free in USA and Canada)
Fax: (336) 272-9015
www.letterarts.com
lar@johnnealbooks.com
Award-winning quarterly magazine for calligraphers and lettering artists

The Lettering Design Group
5830 Nall Avenue, Suite 2
Mission, KS 66202 USA
Telephone: (913) 362-7864
www.spencerian.com
michael@spencerian.com
Calligraphy supplies, videos, books, instruction, and workshops

Mariage Freres
70 Avenue des Terriors de France
75012 Paris, France
Telephone: 33 01 4347 18 54
www.mariagefreres.com
Unbelievable teas from the oldest French importer of teas (their history goes back to the 1660s). Superb blends and styles make a great addition to a gift, a nice selection for a get-together, or a soothing moment for yourself.

Michael's
www.michaels.com

New York Central Art Supply
62 Third Avenue
New York, NY 10003 USA
Telephone: (212) 473-7705 or (800) 950-6111 (Toll free)
www.nycentralart.com
sales@nycentralart.com
Calligraphy, art supplies, books, stationery items, fine papers, frames, mat board

Paper Access
23 West 18th Street
New York, NY 10011 USA
Telephone: (212) 463-7035 or (800) 727-3701 (Toll free)
Fax: (212) 463-7022 or (800) 813-0908 (Toll free)
www.paperaccess.com
info@paperaccess.net
Fine papers, stationery and mailing supplies, ribbon, rubber stamp and embossing supplies, pressed flowers

Paper & Ink Arts
3 North Second Street
Woodsboro, MD 21798 USA
Telephone: (800) 736-7772 or (301) 898-7991
Fax: (888) 736-7773
www.paperinkarts.com or www.paperinkbooks.com
paperinkarts@aol.com or paperinkbk@aol.com
Calligraphy and art supplies, books, fine papers

Paper Source
www.paper-source.com
Locations include Chicago, Cambridge, Minneapolis, and Kansas City (check the website for other cities). Here you'll find papers of all kinds, both luxurious and simple. You'll also find adhesives, book-binding materials, decorations, and other high-quality goods.

Pearl Paint
308 Canal Street
New York, NY 10013 USA
Telephone: (212) 431-7932 or (800) 221-6845 x2297 (Toll free)
www.pearlpaint.com
Calligraphy, art supplies, books, fine papers, pressed flowers, rubber stamp and embossing supplies, frames, mat board

Sam Flax
12 West 20th Street
New York, NY 10011 USA
Telephone: (212) 620-3038 or (800) 726-3529 (Toll free)
www.samflax.com
Calligraphy, art supplies, books, stationery items, fine papers, frames, mat board

Snazzy Bags
www.snazzybags.com

The Society of Scribes & Illuminators
www.calligraphy.org
scribe@calligraphy.org

Staples
www.staples.com

Tender Buttons
143 E. 62nd Street
New York, NY 10021 USA
Telephone: (212) 758-7004
A tiny store can hold quite a lot of buttons—from inexpensive replacements for a white button-down to elaborate and expensive antiques. If you are searching for just the right button to add to a project, they will provide ample choices. With so many beautiful choices, you'll end up leaving with more than you came in for.

Font Libraries

1001 Free Fonts
www.1001freefonts.com

Adobe
Telephone: (800) 833-6687 (Toll free in
USA and Canada)
www.adobe.com

AGFA/Monotype
www.agfamonotype.com
oem.sales@agfamonotype.com

Alphabytes
www.alphabytes.com/calliglinks.html

Brian Hall, Inc.
www.calligraphyfonts.com

The Calligraphy Ring
www.studioarts.net/calligring/index.html

Cynscribe
www.cynscribe.com

Free Fonts on the Web
www.onlinebusiness.com/shops/_
computers/BEST_Fonts.shtml

International Typeface Company
Telephone: (866) 823-5828 (Toll free)
www.itcfonts.com
info@itcfonts.com

Linotype Library
www.linotypelibrary.com
info@fonts.de

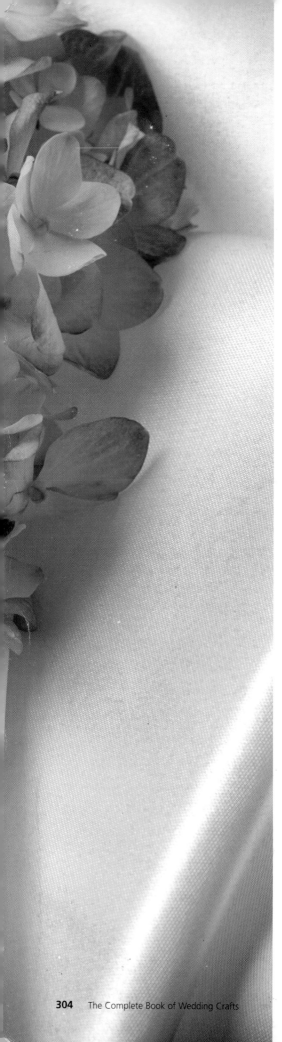

About the Authors

Bette Matthews is the author of *The Wedding Workbook, Cakes (For Your Wedding), Wedding Toasts and Vows,* and *A Wedding for All Seasons.* She has worked as an event consultant and stylist with a New York caterer, and has ventured into designing and producing handmade wedding invitations. Bette lives in New York City with her husband, photographer Antonio M. Rosario, and their three cats.

April L. Paffrath is a freelance editor and writer in Cambridge, Massachusetts. In addition to book and magazine editing, she has written architecture profiles, travel pieces, cooking articles, and craft how-tos for magazines such as *Scientific American Explorations* and *Martha Stewart Living.* She is coauthor of *The Artful Bride: Simple, Handmade Wedding Projects* (Rockport, 2003), *The Artful Bride: Wedding Favors and Decorations* (Quarry Books, 2004), and *The Artful Bride: Wedding Invitations* (Quarry Books, 2004).

Laura McFadden is a freelance art director living in Somerville, Massachusetts. She is a former design director for *Inc.* magazine. She currently runs her own graphic design studio, called Laura McFadden Design, Inc., and has contributed to various craft books and magazines for publishers such as Rockport Publishers, Martingale & Company, and *Handcraft Illustrated.* She is coauthor of *The Artful Bride: Simple, Handmade Wedding Projects* (Rockport, 2003) and *The Artful Bride: Wedding Invitations* (Quarry Books, 2004).

Paula Grasdal is a printmaker and mixed-media artist living in Cambridge, Massachusetts. She has contributed to several Rockport publications and is coauthor of *Collage for the Soul: Expressing Hopes and Dreams through Art* (Rockport, 2003) and *The Artful Bride: Wedding Favors and Decorations* (Quarry Books, 2004).

Livia McRee is a craft writer and designer who is always looking for new twists on beautiful crafts. She lives in San Fransisco, California, and is author of four craft books, including coauthoring *The Artful Bride: Wedding Favors and Decorations* (Quarry Books, 2004).